THE BANKRUPTCY ALTERNATIVE

KEYS TO SUCCESSFUL DEBT SETTLEMENT

A Proven Plan to Work Out Your Debt,
Stop Collectors from Calling You,
and Get Your Life Back

Gregory M. Fitzgerald

The Bankruptcy Alternative
KEYS TO SUCCESSFUL DEBT SETTLEMENT

Gregory M. Fitzgerald, Esq.
Managing Partner at Fitzgerald & Campbell, APLC
400 N. Tustin Avenue, Suite 375
Santa Ana, CA 92705
(855) 709-5788
Gfitzgerald@fclawoffice.com
https://debtorprotectors.com

Expert
Press
www.ExpertPress.net

Table of Contents

What People Say About Greg:

I can not begin to thank you and the attorneys for everything you have done for me. When this first started in January this was an absolute nightmare since I had just had my first baby and dealing with health issues. You guys took this on with such professionalism and confidence and the outcome was even better than I could have imagined. From the bottom of my heart, thank you, thank you ... Thank you.

Know that you made a difference in someone's life. The pressure and anxiety that was lifted each time you reassured me things were being taken care of was priceless. This allowed me to focus my attention on what is most important in my life ... my child and health. I will always think so highly of my experience with Fitzgerald and Campbell as well as YOU.

Thank you.

TINA L., 4/21/2017

5

Excellent law firm! I found them on Yelp and decided to give them a call. I am extremely happy I did. They are very professional, responsive and kept me updated every step of the way. Mr. Fitzgerald is a wonderful person, great attorney and he cares for his clients. This law firm went above and beyond for me and I will always remember their cooperation and amazing results they achieved for me. There are many firms out there that do what they do. Please choose wisely. Not all operate the same and after working with Fitzgerald & Campbell, I understand now why Fitzgerald & Campbell are better than the rest. Give them a call, speak to their nice staff and discuss your issues with them. They are happy to listen and happy to serve. A+ for them for being attorney's with a spine. Thank you Mr. Greg Fitzgerald for everything. I am happy to call you my friend and I am grateful for your excellent service and attention in my case. I will refer anyone that is in the situation I was in, to you and your firm. Keep up the great work sir!

THANK YOU!!!

KAMAL C., 3/17/2017

I found Attorney Fitzgerald of Fitzgerald Campbell, APLC after a simple web search and decided to give his office a call for their free consultation. I had lost my father the year prior and was working my way through severe depression so all my bills had suffered during that time and I was truly overwhelmed by trying to figure things out. The reception was courteous and patient during my initial phone call and all subsequent calls for that matter. I quickly received a return call from Attorney Fitzgerald and we began my initial free consultation. Between the fear, anxiety and stress of my situation, Attorney Fitzgerald was great at keeping me calm and truly hearing me out. Even with my financial situation being shaky, he was reassuring that he would do all he could to help me through it and "we" would work it out. He was very clear on what I needed to do from my side so that he could help me in the best way possible. He answered any and all questions without hesitation and even offered answers to questions I didn't realize I had! The communication with the case managers was and remains clear, concise and quick. Any time I needed some information, they were there. Adam Jauregui and Fabiola Parkerson were great about working within my budget to get started on my cases. Even when I fell behind in my retainer fees due to hard times and moving, they worked with me to get everything on track again. Never once did I feel judged, rushed or pushed into any decision regarding my cases. April Inlow and Sam Foster have been great with keeping me informed about the status of my cases and the honest opinions they had regarding what my options were for my next move in any given situation. I have recently settled the first case and April was great in making sure I was able to get the most realistic payment option within my limits. She communicated with me every step of the way. This is simply an excellent office to work with. I would recommend them to anyone.

LISA, 1/18/17

Table of Contents 7

THE BANKRUPTCY ALTERNATIVE

Introduction

Honestly, it's my opinion that most of those holding themselves out as "debt settlement experts" are not experts at all. Many who proclaim to know it best usually have an agenda that is not consistent with the average consumer who is drowning in debt they can't repay. Nor do I think they really care. They certainly can't relate to the physical and emotional changes your body experiences when you are overwhelmed with all the ramifications that come from unpaid debt. In my opinion the best "experts" are the ones who have personally experienced this and survived to tell their story.

That is why you should not care about my advice about debt relief unless I can do more than provide a "title" or letters after my name, or even who I work for, as the basis for my "expertise." Sure, I am confident in my strategies for debt relief without bankruptcy, but I understand you want more than confidence. You want to know that your "expert" 1) really knows what they are talking about and 2) actually cares about your specific situation. So, let me start by explaining why anyone considering debt settlement for themselves should read this book.

I am an attorney and have been so since 1991. Years of school and nearly 3 decades of lawyering for the "little guy", while certainly useful and important, were not the most important part of my "education" on debt relief generally, and debt settlement specifically. My real education on debt started in 2003. I bought an Irish Pub and the next three years would be the craziest of my life. Long story short, it turns out I'm a much better lawyer than restaurant owner. Thank goodness! I'd much rather be practicing debt settlement than killing myself by running a Pub every day! I should never have gotten involved in an industry I knew very little about. What is important here is that I was ruined financially.

I owed everyone from food and alcohol vendors, credit cards, insurance companies, even ASCAP (for copyrights for the music played in the pub). I was sued many times over and for just about everything you could imagine. I was sued on my Home Depot card. I was sued by American Express, Wells Fargo, and Bank of America to name a few. I was even sued in federal court. I found myself with over $300,000 in unsecured debt. If you can work your way out of that hole, without filing bankruptcy, you can claim to have some expertise in debt settlement. Not that I would wish this kind of 'hands-on' experience on anyone!

It's not a time I like to think about. It's not a time I'm proud of. But it is a time that forged who I was forever to become. I don't blame the creditors at all. They gave me credit and I could not pay them back. The turning point came when I realized that the problem could no longer be ignored, that I could no longer pretend that denial was an effective way to deal with it. The creditors were not going away, and they were a force to be reckoned with!

The good news was, I was a lawyer. I had legal training. I had counseled clients on debt, knew contract law, and knew bankruptcy laws. I had been doing so for 15 years and I was good at it. I had a successful law practice. Using my lawyer training meant taking the emotional component out of the equation. My approach, like that of my creditor counterparts, needed to be strictly business. Absolutely no one cared how or why I owed the money. They just wanted the money. My analysis had to be completely objective. When representing clients, legal training always required an *objective* analysis over a *subjective* one. This first step was huge as it completely took me out of the denial and self-pity that prevented me from the problem-solving approach I always used successfully for my clients.

When I viewed my debt problems objectively, I had to view myself as a client. The first thing I always did with any new client is get the facts. The true facts. What I refer to as the "ultimate facts": Did I owe? Who did I owe? How much did I owe? How fast was it growing? The simple act of putting on paper exactly who I owed and how much actually empowered me because I now knew the size of the problem. Before that, I didn't even want to know. This kept me in the dark and afraid of exactly what I was facing. It was the "boogie man". When it was on paper, the numbers may have been bad, but at least I had a picture of the problem. Many times, when we can't identify the problem, we make it bigger than it really is. Quantifying the problem is the first step of every debt relief plan.

Next was the law: What could creditors do to me? What were my options? Was bankruptcy available to me? Was bankruptcy advisable? What rights do I have? You also must be objective about the law and how judges apply them. Unfortunately, we don't get to apply the laws as we think they should be or would like them to be. This I already knew of course, but it is a lot easier to tell clients "that's the reality" than to accept it for yourself. I also knew the old adage, "The man who represents himself for a client is a fool", was absolutely correct. I did look for an attorney. But all I was told was to "file for bankruptcy". That was not an option for me. I didn't want to jeopardize my home and law practice. Others offered "too good to be true" schemes or "one size fits all" debt negotiators with no real legal training. I was not able to find any reputable attorneys who offered any alternative to bankruptcy. So, I resigned to resolving my own debts myself, knowing that the odds were not in my favor. I was not some brave guy out to show everyone how it's done. I was forced to suck it up to survive. I was not happy about it.

After gathering the facts and applying the appropriate laws, the next thing every good lawyer does is research your opponents and the decision makers. You've got to know who and what you are dealing with. Who are the players? In this industry there are many: the bank, debt collectors, debt buyers, opposing counsel, the judge. How are they going to come after me? When? What can I really settle for? How does the judge come down on these issues?

There were many questions and even less answers. Most people don't know which questions to ask, let alone the answers. And honestly, unless you do it every day, there is no way for you to know all the answers. I don't know all the answers. But I know a lot of them and that is the purpose of this book: to give you the knowledge I learned, much of it the hard way.

If you are unable to pay your debts and are struggling financially, and for whatever reason bankruptcy is not for you, this book will help you to learn what you need to know so you can *best utilize limited resources to maximum effect.* Knowing the Keys to Successful Debt Settlement found in this book will help you to answer questions like: Who do you settle with first? Who is most likely to sue you and when? Do you settle with the debt buyer at a very good rate (but which will take all your available resources, i.e. money) or do you settle with American Express at a higher rate because you know they are more likely to sue you faster?

This book will answer the 10 key questions every person considering debt settlement must ask if they want to complete a successful debt settlement plan:

1. What is a "Debt"?

2. What happens when I default?

3. What are the types of debt and what do the differences mean?

4. What do I need to know about the collection industry?

5. Will I be sued?

6. What are my rights and how do I best apply them?

7. What is the court's role in all this?

8. What is a judgment and what can I do about it?

9. What does a "settlement" really look like?

10. Who is best qualified to create and execute your debt settlement plan?

My sincere hope is that anyone struggling with overwhelming debt will find something useful in this book. Even an answer to one small question might give hope that that there is life after debt. Like many things in life, the first step is often the most difficult. My hope is that by reading this book you will learn that there is some hope for your situation.

This book is not going to guide you on how to do your own debt settlement. Nor is this book going to "sugarcoat" or over simplify the process — debt settlement is not an easy road. It will take time, money and perseverance to successfully complete a debt settlement plan. It will take a well thought out plan based in reality. A plan specific to for your circumstances. A plan based on facts. A plan that incorporates the law as it is actually being applied. Such a plan, in the right hands, can get you debt free. It does work. I know. I did it for myself.

Chapter 1

What are My Debt Relief Options & How Do I Choose?

DEBT RELIEF IS, OR SHOULD BE, STRICTLY ABOUT FINDING THE CHEAPEST WAY OUT OF DEBT. The most effective way to start that process is to talk with someone who completely understands *all* your options and has actually implemented them for others. The best person qualified to do that is a lawyer who practices all aspects of debt relief, bankruptcy and debt settlement. This is the best person to accurately assess your circumstances and be able provide the best advice about your debt relief options.

The Bankruptcy Option

Let's be clear: on a strictly financial analysis, if you are eligible for a Chapter 7 bankruptcy, you should file bankruptcy. In most cases, it is the fastest, cheapest, easiest and, quite frankly, the clearest most indisputable way out of debt. Depending on where you live, the lawyer that you hire for bankruptcy would probably cost between $1,500 or $2,500 for a simple Chapter 7. It takes about four months. Creditors cannot contact you personally, they must stop all collection activity, including lawsuits and judgments. There's no disputing the existence of a court order for discharge (the result of a successful Chapter 7 bankruptcy). If your debt is high and you have no income, bankruptcy is by far the best way to get yourself out of debt and get your family back on its feet for the least cost and in the shortest amount of time.

Like most things in life, there are good and bad aspects to everything. The bad thing about bankruptcy (BK) is that you have a bankruptcy on your credit report. That typically means no credit for at least a year and it will continue to hurt your credit score for several more years. For some jobs or licenses, you can't have a BK. Another drawback to BK is that you are precluded from filing again for 8 years.

Although BK may be your easiest option, it is not automatic. You must qualify for a Chapter 7 BK. In 2005 the bankruptcy laws changed, and it became more difficult to qualify. Although it is much more complicated than this, they created a "means test" that you must pass. This is a financial formula wherein the bankruptcy court looks at the size of your household (how many people live there), and the total gross income that flows into the household. This amount must be below a certain dollar figure in order for you to meet the "presumption" that you qualify for a Chapter 7 bankruptcy.

Remember that the BK "means testing" considers the income for all members of the entire household, even if those other members are not filing BK. The example I use for clients is that my mom lives with me. Altogether there are 4 people in my house. She's on social security. For "means" testing purposes her social security check would be added to my income. Even though my mom wouldn't be filing bankruptcy, her income would be part

THE BANKRUPTCY ALTERNATIVE

of the gross household income. So for an individual to qualify, all income into the household and how many people are in the household is part of the qualification process.

There is also a Chapter 13 Bankruptcy available to consumers. This is generally reserved for those that do not meet the means test or have assets such as a home. This is a very complicated process and involves the debtor making payments to a bankruptcy trustee over many years (typically 5 years) who then makes payments to certain of your creditors pursuant to a court approved "plan".

In truth, a Chapter 13 BK is akin to a debt settlement plan. In the Chapter 13, it is court-controlled process. In debt settlement, its controlled by you (other than to the extent there is a public dispute process at the county courthouse that you can be forced into). But it can be a misnomer for consumers to say they are filing for "bankruptcy protection". The BK court is tasked with protecting creditors as well as debtors. The analysis for a Chapter 13 BK plan is far beyond the scope of this book and you should consult a lawyer before attempting to do a Chapter 13 BK yourself.

The bottom line is, when anyone is looking for debt relief, they need to talk to a lawyer that does BK. Even better, talk to a lawyer that does BK and debt settlement. What I discovered is that most bankruptcy only lawyers will tell you that if you have a debt problem your only option is bankruptcy. That may be good for *them* because that's what they are selling. But that may not always be *your* best option. Therefore, talk to a lawyer that does debt settlement as well as BK.

The Debt Settlement Option

If you have income and/or assets, then debt settlement is something that you should at least investigate. Given the new laws in 2005, many folks no longer qualify for bankruptcy. Therefore, debt settlement is the only other real option to reduce the debt they have. This is also true when you have debts that are generally exempted from bankruptcy (like taxes and student loans) or when bankruptcy is not needed or desired in order to become debt free.

Here's a very simple example of how debt settlement works: Say you have four credit cards with minimum payments of $200 each. If you default on the credit cards (not pay them) and save the $800/mo. instead, in time you will have saved enough money to make a settlement offer of less than 100%. Due to your default, eventually the credit card company will consider less than the full balance as a "settlement in full". That or they will sell or assign the debt to someone who will. Although it's much more complicated than that in actual practice, that is the core of it. For several reasons discussed in more detail later, this should only be done with a lawyer.

As with bankruptcy, debt settlement has its positive and negative elements. When you go the debt settlement route, your credit score will be damaged, just not as badly as in BK. It will dive, but it will also recover when the debts are settled because, unlike Chapter 7 BK, you are going to pay the creditor something. Debt settlement gives you time, but it is a debt workout, and a workout means work. It could take months and even years. You will pay money. With a Chapter 7 BK you'll give your creditors zero dollars. With debt settlement, you will give them some amount of money (although not always), so clearly it costs more dollars out of your pocket to do a debt settlement plan than a bankruptcy. With debt settlement your credit score recovers faster because you paid the creditor something.

One of the challenges to debt settlement is you must be aware of the many myths and abuses by non-lawyer operators (and even some lawyer operations) that are scams. There a lot of "consumer advocates" that are selling snake oil frauds like "debt elimination" scams and many others. But even the honest non-lawyer debt settlement companies (DSC) should be avoided as they are not going to be able to advise you on all your options, let alone be able to implement all your options. For example, you may start a debt settlement plan because you are working. If you lose your job, you may need to change the plan to a BK. No DSC is going to be able to determine that for you, let alone file a BK for you. Another example is that every debt settlement plan includes a chance you will be sued. No DSC can assist you with that. Finally, as discussed in more detail below, DSCs cannot assist you with harassment claims or even stop the collection calls.

What About "Debt Consolidation" as an Option?

"Debt Consolidation" is another term that is improperly used, mostly by debt settlement companies. DSC salespersons often refer to their services as "debt consolidation". This is an out and out deception. Debt Settlement is not a consolidation of your debts, but they many times lead consumers to believe that is what they have done. The ruse is that you pay the DSC one amount per month, and the DSC pays all your creditors, so it sounds and feels like a debt consolidation. That simply is not the case at all. Your debts have not been "consolidated" in the least by your DSC. Individual creditors can, and will, still pursue you.

True debt consolidation occurs when you get a <u>new loan that pays off all the other debts</u>. Many times this is done as part of a refinance or as a federal student loan consolidation. The new loan pays off all the old loans leaving you with one new loan and one new payment. Usually you can get a lower interest rate or a longer payment term. This can be a very helpful debt relief approach. One negative is that when done as part of a refinance on your home, the debt is now secured by the house. Accordingly, you have turned an unsecured debt into a secured debt. Generally, that is a bad idea.

One positive of debt consolidation via refinance use to be that the interest was tax deductible. Be advised that such is not necessarily the case under the new Trump tax plan.

True debt consolidation does have a place. If you can get a new loan at a better rate and pay it off, and satisfy all your other creditors, it can be useful. I've done it myself, and I may do it again. But don't be fooled by the terminology used by non-reputable debt settlement companies. Be aware that you're turning debt from unsecured debt into secured debt, which has ramifications and costs that you need to consider.

What About Credit Counseling?

The thing to consider about credit counseling is – Does the counselor get paid anything by the creditors? If so, you have to ask yourself: who are they really working for? Are they working for you or are they working for who pays them? You *hope* they're working for you. Some get paid by both the consumer and the bank. But if you're not paying a credit counselor, often they are working for the *other* side. While they are trying to find a way that you can afford your payments, there is no debt reduction.

Another thing to keep in mind is that when you use a credit counselor, you have no principal savings. You're not going to get actual debt relief. You might get an easier payment and you might get a lower interest rate, but you will pay 100% of the debt because you will pay the entire amount of the debt. It's not really a debt reduction option, but it does have a place and can be what some people need.

Who Can You Trust to Help You Make the Right Decision?

As you consider your options, I would strongly suggest that you consider consulting with an attorney who is skilled in protecting all your rights as a consumer. You need a lawyer who is a master of debt relief—someone who knows bankruptcy, debt settlement, collection lawsuits, judgments, and collection harassment. Someone who files collection harassment cases against collectors. Someone who defends collection lawsuits. Someone who can help you develop a successful plan, be it a Chapter 7 or 13 or debt settlement. Someone who can provide all the services that may be required in a debt relief plan today, and next year when your circumstances may change. Someone who knows all your options AND can apply them all, will not "advise" you based upon their own self-interests (that is, only "sell" you on what they are "selling").

There are some other even more obvious reasons to never consider advice from a non-lawyer for your debt relief plan: A DSC not only can't file bankruptcy (BK), but collectors know that a DSC does not want you to file BK because the DSC will lose you as customer. This knowledge by the collector significantly hinders the best possible settlement for the consumer who uses a DSC or non-BK law firm.

Another important distinction is that a non-lawyer debt settlement company cannot stop the telephone calls. They cannot stop a consumer's collectors from calling them. In CA, a good debt relief lawyer can actually stop the calls. Even calls from the original creditor. A non-lawyer cannot file harassment claims. A lawyer can file harassment lawsuits on your behalf. Collectors know this and therefore are less likely to make improper calls and other harassment, like name-calling, misstating debt, or calling you after 9:00 at night.

Further, only a lawyer can defend you in court if a collector takes you to court. A DSC will settle at all costs (usually resulting in a higher settlement) because the DSC can do nothing to stop the lawsuit. When a collector threatens me with a lawsuit, I say "don't threaten me with a good time. I will happily see you in court. Besides, if you sue, you will lose your commission, and nobody will be paid for months, even years. And then we will file BK." You can see how this is much more effective than "please don't sue my customer".

Those are the three biggest tools (BK, collection harassment protection, defending collection lawsuits) that a consumer has in terms of fighting back against a creditor. When you don't use a lawyer, you've given up the three biggest tools available to you. And you don't have enough tools as it is!

There's an even more practical reason to only use a lawyer: If for some reason you have a dispute with your lawyer, the lawyer is licensed, and the lawyer is very concerned about that license. You can contact the state's Bar Association to complain about that lawyer. A lot of people have been ripped off by debt settlement companies that took the client's money and never settled their debts. Maybe they even closed their doors. They are left chasing a debt settlement company, maybe from another state, who's been shut down by the government. Not a good place to be when you can merely contact the state bar to report attorney misconduct. Even better: the CA state bar maintains a fund to pay victims of lawyer abuse.

Finally, when you hire a non-lawyer debt settlement company, you enter a contract agreement. That means that both sides are "equal" and its "buyer beware". The DSC can go to that contract and say, "Look, we told them, we disclosed it. They checked the box. We're not responsible." If you have that situation with a lawyer, the lawyer will lose that argument every single time because it is not a buyer beware type of contract. It is a "retainer agreement" and the attorney has a fiduciary obligation to put you first. It is an entirely different relationship where the lawyer must put your interests above their own. That is just not so for a DSC/customer relationship.

For all these reasons and more, a good debt relief lawyer is your best option to determine the best way to debt relief for you and your family. They can modify your plan. They can tailor make your plan, they can assert all consumer rights, and you the consumer have more protections.

If it is debt settlement that is the option for you, the rest of this book will be very helpful to understand exactly all that is involved in debt settlement.

THE BANKRUPTCY ALTERNATIVE

Chapter 2:

Getting Started on a Debt Settlement Plan: "Debt" Basics

For purposes of explanation, when we talk about a "debt" in this book, we are assuming you concede that an amount is due. In my debt relief practice I never make this assumption. I always start with the view that a creditor's claim is merely that: "a claim" only. To say it is a "debt" concedes money is due. In the legal world, nothing is decided until a court rules on it. Prior to that, the parties are all making allegations and claims that are not yet proven. Perhaps more importantly, these "claims" cannot be enforced (no money seized) without court assistance.

The "Life of a Debt" Overall:

The first thing that you need to know about the life of a debt is that a debt will continue to exist until: 1) it's paid (settled qualifies so long as properly documented), or 2) is discharged in a bankruptcy. If one of those two things do not happen, it continues to exist (in California) in some form, forever.

What many people don't realize is that when you stop paying a "debt", your legal position, over time, actually becomes stronger and the creditor's position becomes weaker. I refer to the period of time between default (when you are supposed to make a payment but do not) and the filing of a lawsuit on the claim (which may never happen) as the account's "pregnancy". The unpaid debt will give birth to a lawsuit or it won't. The debt will have two very different "lives" depending upon if an unpaid debt goes "full term" (a lawsuit is filed in the court) or not.

Let me explain. When you default on a debt, there are only three things a creditor can do. One, they can call you and write you letters and ask (demand?) to be paid. If you have a lawyer, they can't do that anymore because they have to talk to your lawyer. Two, they can negatively impact your credit. Three, they can file a lawsuit asking the court for a decision that it is, in fact, a debt you owe. Those are the only three things they can do to you. If they do not sue you (no "birth" of a lawsuit), they are left only with the first two options to collect.

Another way to look at it is when you default, two "clocks" begin to run. The first clock is the statute of limitations – the time that the creditor must go to court to initiate a lawsuit against you. If that clock runs out, they lose the right to "win" in court. In California that's a four-year clock for most unsecured debts, although there are exceptions. You want that four-year clock to start running as soon as possible and to keep running. If it runs out and they don't sue you, you can never be forced to pay them any money. I have many clients that never get sued on "a claim". Because the creditor is on this "clock" their legal position is weakening over time and the consumer position is getting stronger.

If you don't get sued, keep in mind that when year 5 rolls around, you still "owe" the money. The "debt" is still alive and collectible. The creditor has only lost the one collection tool of a lawsuit. They have not lost the right to collect money from you. They have not lost the right to ask for payment. They have not lost the right to report you to credit bureaus. They have only lost the mechanism of a lawsuit to force payment.

The second clock that runs is the seven-year reporting clock on your credit report. When you don't pay a debt, it can be reported on your credit report for up to 7 years. After that it comes off. But as before, in year 8 you still "owe" the debt. It didn't just go away because they can't report it anymore. They can still call you (so long as you have no lawyer). They can still ask to be paid, because the debt still exists. They've just lost the right to report it. At this point there's not much reason to pay them into years eight, nine, ten and beyond because they cannot force payment and they cannot report you to the credit bureaus. Over time the consumer's tools (rights) get stronger. On the other hand, the creditors' tools (or rights) to collect the debt begin to diminish with time.

You should also know that when they lose these rights, not only do they lose the right, but they also lose the threat of asserting that right. For example, as stated above, in year five they've lost the right to win in court. If they know the statute of limitations has passed and threaten to sue you or do things they no longer have the legal right to do such as garnish your wages, they have committed collection harassment and you have a claim against them for violation of collection laws.

Life of a Debt when Default leads to the "Birth" of a Lawsuit (Statute of Limitations "clock" does not run out)

There are 3 stages in the life of a debt that goes to court:

1. Default Stage (account becomes "pregnant"): The first stage is after default, but before the lawsuit. Some debts never go beyond stage 1 because they get settled before a lawsuit is filed or the creditor just does not sue. In our experience, less than 18% of defaulted credit card accounts end up in court. There are many factors such as who you are financially, who is the creditor, the type of debt, etc. During this stage creditors will demand payment, threaten lawsuits (and all the things that flow from lawsuit judgments like wage garnishments, bank levies, etc.), and report your delinquency to the credit bureaus. The thing to remember at this stage is that it is just a claim. As I stated above, I don't like to even call it a debt. I don't like to call it collection. I don't like to call it anything but a third-party claim. It has not yet been proven. It has not been determined you owe it. It's simply a claim for money. I might as well write you a letter and say you owe me money. It means nothing more than that and has no force of law behind it.

2. Lawsuit Stage ("pregnant" account has given "birth" to a lawsuit): The second stage is when they file a lawsuit against you. Now you must act. You cannot ignore a lawsuit. Well, you can ignore a lawsuit, but you *should* not. Many clients might claim they weren't served correctly so they'll ignore the case. That's a bad approach. You should respond to a lawsuit even if you feel it was not served correctly.

A lawsuit does not necessarily mean that you owe the money. Many people readily admit that they "owe" the money. While I appreciate the honesty, I tell them: litigation is not about whether you owe the money. Other than as an ultimate goal, no lawsuit is about the truth of the matter. Litigation is about what can be proven. It's "put up or shut up" time. Litigation is the process by which the courts seek the correct "outcome" or "justice". However, many times the process takes precedence over the "truth" and therefore cases become less about what really happened and more about who can navigate the litigation process better.

We recently had a trial on a student loan case filed by a debt buyer. They purchased a student loan totaling $17,000 and decided to sue our client. When we went to trial, the debt buyer presented evidence, but they didn't prepare properly and there was a defect in their evidence. The judge said from the bench, "Even though I believe your client owes the money, plaintiff did not properly present their case and therefore I proclaim a verdict in favor of the defendant." Our client paid no money because the claimant didn't follow the proper process. They did not adequately "prove their case". They didn't present their evidence in the proper way. Everyone knew our client had borrowed the money, but it didn't matter. The student defendant won. Did the student "owe" the money? Yes. Are they going to pay the money? No.

Moral of the story is don't assume you will lose the case just because you "owe" the debt. Likewise, if you *don't* owe the money, do not assume you will win. Just like we have clients that owe and don't pay, there are consumers that do not actually owe the money who end up paying.

I always tell my clients to be realistic. Is litigation always about what really happened? No. However, don't think that means you don't have to pay. You haven't won it yet. For instance, some may think, "Hey, this is a debt buyer who is suing me. I don't really owe this person. I don't even know who they are." The law does allow for debts to be bought and sold and you can be ordered to pay someone other than the original creditor you owed the money to.

That's why we strongly suggest that you enter this phase with someone who knows the litigation process like a good debt relief attorney with litigation experience. One who understands the process. One who knows the evidence code. One who knows what it takes to represent you well. Chapter 8 is dedicated to collection lawsuits.

3. Judgment Stage (the "baby", the debt, is in fact yours– even if it ain't!): If you lose the case, the litigated "claim" has now reached the third and last stage: judgment. A judgment is a court order that says you owe a certain sum of money to a specific person or entity. When a claim has become a judgment, it now has the power of the court behind it. It is now a true debt. The judge can then order you and others (such as employers, banks, others) to turn over your money to the judgment creditor. They are no longer "claimants" but are judgment creditors. It does not matter whether you actually "owed" it or not, you must pay it. Chapter 9 is dedicated to Judgments.

Where you are on this continuum in the life of a debt that goes to court is important. You must accurately determine where you are with all your accounts, be it a "claim", a lawsuit, or a judgment/court order. Your plan must recognize the stage of each debt as this will have a direct impact on your overall debt settlement plan success.

Additional Basics You Must Know for a Successful Debt Settlement Plan

Once you have determined which stage a debt is in, you need to determine what law applies at the various stages. This is what I refer to as the weapons, or the tool belt, that you have as a consumer. Beware of the myths that you may have heard. If you think that you have a tool in your tool belt and it's really a plastic toy, you will only hurt yourself and jeopardize your entire debt settlement plan.

One such myth is commonly referred to as "debt elimination". There is no debt elimination other than bankruptcy or payment. Anybody who says you can eliminate your debts by writing a letter to your creditor is a scam. There's no other word for it. Don't fall for someone who says you can buy your own debts or claims they will buy your debt and pay them instead. Those are all scams.

If you attempt to assert a right you really don't have, you will lose. The judge will roll his/her eyes. The collection lawyer will laugh. The collector will laugh even harder. You know what? They have every right to, because you're now throwing things at them that mean nothing. It shows your ignorance. It makes you an easy mark.

The tools that you *do* have can be effective. You don't need the myths. For example, there is the FDCPA, which stands for Fair Debt Collection Practices Act. It's a federal law most people are familiar with in terms of protecting consumers from collectors. It can be a very powerful law so long as it is asserted *correctly*. The best way (only way?) to do that is with a qualified lawyer. More on this very important consumer tool in Chapter 7.

There are many misconceptions about what is sometimes referred to as debt validation or verification. Many times people write to the creditor demanding "proof of the debt". If they don't get it, they assume they can't be forced to pay. Wrong. That only applies in the courtroom. You can demand proof, but the creditor's failure to provide it does not mean the debt has been eliminated. I wish that were true, but it just isn't. Debt validation and its application and usefulness as a tool is perhaps the most widely understood myth about debt relief, perpetuated mostly by scam "consumer advocates" selling too good to be true cures.

The statute of limitation is another great law for consumers. Was the lawsuit filed within the statute or outside the statute? Again, going back to the life of a debt, you need to know what stage it's at and how long. Applied properly, the statute of limitations can prevent claims from ever becoming lawsuits and judgments.

The nuclear weapon you have (if you qualify) is BK. Sometimes the mere threat of BK, just like bomb, can be an adequate deterrent. In the hands of an experienced attorney who knows how to use it, BK threats can be very effective. That said, even the BK tool, if improperly applied can have a negative effect on your debt settlement plan. For example, if you threaten a creditor with BK, and you had successfully completed a BK two years ago, your creditor will know you can't file BK again and that you are ignorant of the law or worse, that you are bluffing. Your "bomb" has just blown up in your face!

Creditors must make certain disclosures to you required by state and federal laws. Do you know what they are? If they don't provide those disclosures, they have violated those laws. That doesn't mean *you* automatically get your debt wiped out. It only means *they* pay a penalty (assuming you can prove your "claim" to a judge or at least convince the collector you will be able to do so). Do you think the collector believes that you, on your own, will ever be able to prove that to a judge? Heck no.

Nor is getting the collector to pay a penalty for violating the FDCPA equal to debt relief. They could pay you the penalty and you still owe the debt. If you have a $30,000 Capital One account, and they violate the FDCPA by contacting you incorrectly, you still owe $30,000 dollars. They may have to give you $1,000 dollars, but you still owe the $30,000 dollars. In order to get rid of the $30,000 debt, those tools need to be used correctly. A lot of lawyers can't do it correctly, let alone you on your own. I've done it. As explained in more detail in Chapter 7, not using a lawyer on your FDCPA case will gut your case because it is the attorney fees they may have to pay that worries them, not the $1,000 penalty.

Lastly, understanding the life of the debt means you need to understand the creditors rights as much as the consumers rights. The creditor has many rights and unless you are knowledgeable about these rights, they will run right over you. For example, you should know collectors have more options than just a breach of contract case against you. They have non-contract theories of recovery. So even if they don't have a physical contract, they can still collect money.

Assume I am a gardener and let's say I don't have a written contract with my customer. My customer refuses to pay saying "show me the contract". The customer still owes me the money and can be forced to pay. I can still collect the reasonable value of my services. Creditors do the same. They tell the judge, quite legally and quite successfully, "Your Honor, we don't have a copy of the contract. We do have a series of transactions where this consumer went to Target or Walmart and they used their Capital One account to purchase it. They should not get those things for free, even though we don't have a physical contract." The court will agree, and that is the law. People get caught up on written contracts. Collectors don't have to have a written contract to win a case against you.

Creditors also have a right to sell, assign, or transfer your debt "obligation" to another. They don't have to keep them. Many people don't think debts can be sold. Debts are bought and sold on a regular basis and they have the absolute right to do it. Same with judgments.

Creditors also have the right to report to credit bureaus. They have a right to contact you and ask to be paid. They have a right to contact third parties to locate you. The reason you put a reference on an application is so they can call that reference to locate you. These are all very powerful rights that creditors have. And they will use them against you.

Finally, there are different types of creditors and different laws apply to them. For this reason, you must know who the creditors are as you consider your plan. For example, there are two types of "original creditors" and the laws are very different depending on who you are dealing with. Some original creditors are in the business of lending money such as Bank of America, Wells Fargo, and so forth. Those entities regularly engage in debt collection. They lend money and if people don't pay them back, they collect it. A large part of Bank of America's business is to collect debts. I generally refer to these types of original creditors as institutional lenders.

You have other original creditors who are not in the business of collecting, such as your dentist. Your dentist has provided a service. If you don't pay your dentist, your dentist is going to want to be paid. What's important about the distinction is that your dentist is not a "debt collector" as that term is defined by the law. He's a business trying to get paid for services rendered. He's not in the business of debt collecting. You do not have FDCPA collection harassment rights against your dentist.

Now that you have a handle on some of the basics of debt, you need to know more about the specific type(s) of debts you have. This is because different laws apply to different types of debts.

Chapter 3

Type of Debt I: Consumer Debts

Your overall debt relief plan will depend on the type, or types, of debt you have. Many plans will have to deal with different types of debts. The most common debt type is consumer debt.

Know the Difference between a consumer and commercial debt:

Consumer debts are transactions that are primarily for personal, family, or household purposes. This contrasts with a business/commercial debt that arises out of a commercial transaction. There are very different laws for both the creditor and the debtor that depend upon this distinction. The reason for this is that in consumer transactions there is presumed an "unequal bargaining position": consumer versus the bank; consumer versus a large business; consumer versus an insurance company. For this reason, laws provide more protections for the consumer. When it comes to commercial transactions, it's a business to business transaction where it is presumed the parties are on a more equal footing. Therefore, the protections are different. The laws that protect <u>people</u> from collection harassment, such as the FDCPA, do not apply to your business debts. It only applies to consumer debts. That's also why consumer debt is generally easier to resolve than business debt (more tools are available to fight with).

The first thing a judge is going to do in every single case, trial, or hearing is decide what law applies. It's not always clear whether the transaction is a consumer transaction or a business transaction, so you need to provide evidence to prove it one way or the other.

Whether a debt is commercial or consumer is not always determined by your credit card account type. Nor is it determined by the account's name. For example, you might have a business credit card and a personal credit card. That's not the determining factor. What matters is the actual transaction itself. What was the purchased product or service used for? If you went out and bought flowers for your wife on your commercial credit card, that's a consumer transaction. If on your consumer credit card, you went out and purchased a piece of equipment, such as a printer for your business, that would be a commercial transaction. It's determined by the nature of the transaction or the nature of the purchase. As the consumer, that is the kind of evidence you will need to provide.

Once you determine that the transaction is of the consumer variety, there are many types of consumer transactions (i.e.: medical, student loans, credit card, auto) which, again, the laws will vary on.

Medical Debt

Medical debt is perhaps the easiest to identify as a consumer debt. I want to emphasize that these laws change constantly, and no book can replace the advice of a one-on-one conversation with an attorney. That said, let me give you an idea of what you should consider when developing a debt settlement plan that includes medical debt.

Even though it is common, medical debt is very tricky because insurance companies and government regulations play an integral role in what you may owe. Insurance companies are in the business of collecting premiums and minimizing claims. They are for profit enterprises and make business decisions, not health care decisions. We commonly assist clients in getting their insurance companies to pay claims that have been denied. They play an integral part in medical debt and therefore are usually involved when trying to complete a debt settlement plan.

The laws on payment of medical debt are different than other types of consumer debt. Generally, there is no written contract. Never do you see an itemized list of fees and charges BEFORE services are rendered. There might be a signed agreement between you and the physician, or the hospital, or other medical provider. But these agreements are mostly about accepting responsibility for payment and limiting the medical providers liability. But there isn't a contract that says you're going to pay a $100 for a blood transfusion or a blood test or anything else. There's no written agreement with specific terms. There is absolutely no ability to negotiate these terms in advance of services. Nor is there the option to shop providers (other than perhaps what insurance company you go with).

What's important to know is that the medical provider can only charge what's reasonable and necessary. While this is bad if you'd like to know what you are getting into before the fact, it is good when it comes to negotiating the amount of a debt after the fact. Without a written contract there is room for debate on what is reasonable and necessary.

Here's a typical example. I had a client with a $70,000 medical bill for a six hour stay. He had an automobile accident but felt he didn't need to go in the ambulance to the hospital. The ambulance took him anyway, and during his brief stay at the hospital, they ran a series of tests on him. They released him the same day and allowed him to walk home, which was about ten miles. Essentially, they charged him $70,000 for some tests. Unfortunately, that is too common. Who really knows whether he needed the tests or not? I don't know. The client may have approved them. As his attorney, my goal was to gather the evidence and determine if the charges were reasonable and necessary. This is not always easy. On its face, it seems outrageous, but good medical care does have costs. The client did not pay anything near that amount.

I had another client who was skiing in the mountains and had a heart attack. He was flown by a medical evacuation airplane to the closest hospital. He received an airplane bill for more than $40,000. I spoke to his wife and she said, "had we known it was going to be $40,000, we may have elected to drive the two hours down the mountain." But there was no contract up front to explain the cost of traveling by air to get to the hospital. Even the medical providers often have no idea what the charges will be. The paramedics are making many individual medical decisions on the fly (no pun intended). Do you need this test? Do you need that intervention? Should we get this? Should we use that? There is no clear-cut answer. Many of us would have to admit that as the patient, we'd rather be over tested than under tested.

Others may want an abundance of caution. It is a balancing act that often doesn't end up very balanced. Worse, when those decisions are being made, you the patient or family member are not thinking of the financial consequences.

In the end, there are many legitimate issues regarding whether the treatment was necessary, and the charges were reasonable. It becomes even more complex because many times the medical provider will charge the insurance company one amount, and you as an individual a different amount. Medical debt can be complex, confusing, and massive. And just like any other consumer debt, you need to fight hard on these cases to be successful.

We had another client with approximately $35,000 medical bill from the county hospital. He had been stabbed at his company's Christmas party. There were all sorts of issues from health insurance to worker's compensation insurance, to indigent medical services (state assistance). The county hospital sued, and it was set for trial. My client never denied that there was some amount of money that he owed, and he wanted to pay. He just didn't have $35,000. But the hospital wouldn't accept anything less than that and they wouldn't accept a payment plan.

The client had little to lose by taking the case to trial. The worst that could happen is a court ruling that he did owe the $35,000. But the week before the trial, the hospital dismissed the case. We found out from the hospital's counsel that they were not going to be able to have a witness show up at the trial. The county hospital dismissed the case, and our client paid nothing. Even better, the county reimbursed our client his legal fees. Fighting these cases, even when you concede you owe something, can get you positive results and have a dramatic impact on your overall plan to become debt free.

An issue we frequently encounter on medical debt is consumers who pay the medical bill with their credit card. I strongly urge you *not* to do this. You'll lose all the medical bill defenses that you might have. When you pay your medical bill with your credit card, you can no longer contest the amount as unreasonable or unnecessary. Let's say you have a $6,000 doctor bill that you paid with your Discover card. Later you decide that the bill really should have been closer to $2,000. If you're trying to settle with Discover, they won't care what the money was used for. They only care that they paid the $6,000 to the doctor. They will correctly claim that you should have talked to the doctor if you thought they were charging too much for their services. And they will be right. In a Discover card lawsuit, the court will not go through your medical bills to see if the charges were reasonable and necessary. It is never a good plan to pay disputed medical bills with your credit card.

Credit Card Debt

This is the most common type of consumer debt. Almost everyone has had a credit card. The majority of these are consumer transactions. While they are simple and straightforward in concept, there are a lot of regulations and laws. Anyone looking to settle credit card debt needs to be up to speed on these laws.

Unmanageable credit card debt is generally seen as something where you didn't manage your finances correctly. Sometimes this is true and sometimes it isn't. Truth is, from a debt settlement point of view, it does not matter. You made charges at the bookstore, and now you owe the money.

The reality is a lot of people pay their bills with their credit cards when they lose their job and unemployment benefits are not enough. The credit card is a great tool to bridge a financial hardship. They can also be used to start a business or get you through a business cash flow problem. But they can get to be quite expensive. As the simplest type of consumer debt, it's the one that most often gets consumers and small businesses into trouble.

Still, if you're going to have any type of debt, the debt that you want to have is credit card debt. It's among the easiest to resolve because consumers have the most rights.

Auto Repossessions

The following thoughts are assuming that the car was not a commercial vehicle used for business.

Amounts due after an auto repossession are what car lenders and attorneys refer to as "deficiency cases". Let's say you purchased a car and got a $20,000 loan. You've made payments for a few years so that now you may have a balance of $15,000. For whatever reason you can't continue making your payments. The bank comes along and repossesses the car. They will add the repossession costs on to your balance. They'll often add on refurbishing costs, like rekeying the automobile, since they're not going to resell it with the same key that you have. By the time they add late fees and interest, your balance due may be closer to $18,000.

Then they will sell the car at an auction, typically a wholesale auction for dealers where they will not get retail value. Say they get $10,000. This will be applied to the $18,000 due which means you now owe $8,000. That's the "deficiency" that they will try to collect from you.

You might be upset because the car was only sold for $10,000, even though it was worth $15,000. While that may be true, the lender can sell these cars at an auction. The good news is that there are very strict laws that the lender must follow to repossess an auto and pursue you for any deficiency balance. When you do have a vehicle that has been repossessed, any debt settlement plan must have a solid understanding of all the applicable laws in order to settle for the lowest possible balance. These lenders do make mistakes as the repossession laws are very specific.

For instance, after they repossess a vehicle, they must give you notice and an opportunity to cure. That means they must give you an opportunity to pay the past due balance as well as any late fees or charges. If you do, you can get the vehicle back. You have a right to that. If they don't send you that letter, and don't give you that opportunity, they've violated the repossession statutes. They also must give you an inventory of what's in the car and give you an opportunity to get your personal effects out of the car. They must also give you the breakdown of the deficiency (what they sold the car for). Some of these notices must be sent by certified mail.

Many lenders don't follow this process to a T, and if there's a defect in that process, that repossession is defective. It's very important to have a legal expert who knows the process and who's done it before as it can save you a lot of money and make your overall debt settlement plan even more effective.

Important note about "voluntary" repossessions and "lemons":

There's a myth (often perpetuated by banks & collectors) commonly called a "voluntary repo". This is where a person returns the vehicle voluntarily by driving the car back to the lender or the dealer and turning over the keys. You might think that is not a repossession and therefore you will owe nothing because you returned the vehicle voluntarily. Unfortunately, that's just not true. It's still a repossession and there is absolutely no difference in terms of what you may owe (other than there will be no repo man fees added to your deficiency because you actually gave it back to them).

Most clients who voluntarily turn their car in tell me that they called the bank and the bank said, "If you turn it in, there probably won't be any deficiency and we won't go after you." They say that so that you turn it in. Once you turn it in, they are required by law to follow the exact same process on any repossession. The bottom line? The repossession statutes make no difference between voluntary or involuntary repos.

Another myth about auto repossessions involves lemons. The car may not work correctly, so a consumer might think, "If it doesn't work, I don't have to pay." That's wrong. Your agreement with your lender is separate from your purchase agreement for the car. Just because the car was a lemon or was misrepresented, (i.e.: faulty performance or odometer readings), that's a case you have against the <u>seller</u>. The lender has no part of that transaction, and they still have a right to pursue payments from you, and if they so choose, repossess the vehicle. If you try to assert lemon law defenses in a deficiency case in court, the judge, who is the only person we care about, will just roll his/her eyes.

When I first started my practice, I represented many used car dealers. I did a lot of deficiency cases for used car dealers who made their own loans to consumers. This a very specific area of the law. Winning or losing a case such as this is directly related to knowing the very specific legal requirements. Again, you need to know more than the collector to be successful.

Payday/Installment/Online Loans

This type of consumer debt is becoming more common. They often have outrageously high interest rates. I saw one that had an interest rate of 428%. The truth is, I generally tell people not to pay them. The typical collection model for these lenders is to *not* file lawsuits. Payday lenders, like the aggressive and predatory nature of their loans, take that same business ethic into their collection model. Essentially it is harassment. They will call you incessantly to collect any amount of money, and they will jack up the number from $300 to $5,000, all as a scare tactic to get people to pay them. I tell people not to pay them because you can do better in court, even *if* they sue you. We generally tell these lenders, "Go away. We don't have any intention of paying you. If you want to take us to court, we're happy to see you in court. We're happy to see you explain to the judge the 428% interest rate." That is not to say that these contracts are illegal on their face. They can be "legal", but generally judge's do not like them, and they are more receptive to good arguments about misrepresentations and defective terms.

They do however have no problem calling and calling and calling consumers. Payday loans are predatory and real problematic. If you want to stop the calls, you really need to have a good lawyer. These lenders provide many of the best collection harassment lawsuits we file. We've had them pay damages many times, but they are going to continue because they accept they may have to pay damages to the few consumers who smartly got good lawyers. Unfortunately, they will still collect far more money than they will ever pay out for violating collection harassment laws. It is like the Ford Pinto case. Ford knew the Pinto gas tank was dangerous and people had died because of its faulty design. Worse, despite knowing that more may die, they decided not to fix it. It was cheaper to pay a few wrongful death claims than to fix the problem on thousands of Pintos.

Finally, there are many payday lenders that are based within Indian reservations across the nation. I especially tell people not to pay those loans, because they almost never sue you. On behalf of clients, we have sued Indian Tribes for collection harassment. Most Tribes don't ever defend them. I have obtained judgments against Indian reservations because they are subject to the state and federal laws where they do business. However, the trouble is that a California judgment against them is worthless because it is not enforceable inside the tribal lands.

Foreclosures on Your Residence

A *second* mortgage is still collectable, even if your home has been foreclosed upon unless the loan was "purchase money" (money received was used to purchase the property). Most people think, "I've had a non-judicial foreclosure. I no longer owe the banks." That's true on your first mortgage, but not automatically so on the second mortgage or HELOC, or any other lenders that may have recorded a lien against your home, such as judgment liens and HOA fees.

Subrogation Claims- Insurance

If you are at fault for an automobile collision and you have no insurance (or not enough), the individual who you hit will probably make a claim against their own insurance company (an "uninsured/underinsured motorist" claim) and have their insurance company pay them. When this happens, that insurance company has the right to pursue you for the amounts they paid to their own insured. This is called Subrogation. It is most common with automobile insurance but also occurs in other types of insurance cases like workers compensation, property damage claims, etc. And it applies to more than just uninsured consumers. It also applies to *underinsured* consumers.

A good example is an uninsured client who rear ended a pizza delivery man. The pizza delivery man was driving his own vehicle, but he was within the course and scope of his employment. He filed a claim for the damage to his vehicle. He also made a worker's compensation claim against the pizza company. Both the vehicle insurer and the workers' compensation insurance company, who paid the guy for his damages, pursued my client for reimbursement of everything they paid out on the claim.

Like anything else, these types of claims can be negotiated. They can and should be a part of any debt settlement plan, but you've got to have the right lawyer who knows how that works. Insurance laws can be very particular in terms of how clients must make their claims, how they must assert the claims. A collection law specific to these debts are that judgments against uninsured drivers can also result in suspension of one's driver's license until paid. Another one is that registered owners of the auto can also be held responsible (up to a certain amount) even though they were not driving the car or even in the car.

HOA–Homeowners Association Disputes

It is common for a resident to be fined by their HOA. These have been ruled to be a consumer debt.

Attorney Fee Disputes

In the course of life, sometimes people have to hire lawyers. In today's society it would be very difficult to never need the services of a lawyer at some point. Be it a divorce, accident, small business venture, or an employment law issue, legal disputes happen, and lawyers become necessary. This inevitably leads to disputes over legal fees. Attorney fee disputes are just another type of debt that can be either consumer or commercial and should be a part of any debt settlement plan if you have a lawyer or other professional alleging you owe them money. In California, before a lawyer can sue a client they must give them an opportunity to arbitrate. As amazing as it sounds, many lawyers don't know or don't follow that requirement, and they'll institute an action against the consumer improperly. Unfortunately, some also have a propensity to overbill and bully clients for payment.

Not too long ago, we did an attorney fee arbitration for a business client. Attorneys were pursuing our client for $7,000 in "unpaid" legal fees. The arbitrator ruled in our client's favor and ordered that the attorneys reimburse our client for overcharged fees, pay our client's attorney fees to complete the arbitration as well as our client's arbitration costs. The attorneys ended up paying our client $20,000 when they were seeking $7,000 from our client. Having the right lawyer who knows the law and won't be bullied can make a huge difference in resolving attorney fee claims.

THE BANKRUPTCY ALTERNATIVE

Chapter 4

Type of Debt II: Commercial Debts

Simply put, a commercial debt must arise from a commercial transaction. As stated above, the biggest difference between consumer debts and commercial debts is that consumer protection laws do not apply to commercial debts. For example, there is actually no statutory law preventing a vendor of your business from calling you at 10pm or using profanity.

Also, there are fewer legal protections in commercial loan agreements and transactions because fewer disclosures are required. The protections against predatory loans, or disclosure laws, that you see for consumer debt are not as common when it comes to commercial debt. That's because the state views a commercial transaction as "business-to-business" and generally a "buyer beware" transaction. That can lead to a lot of abuses in commercial loan agreements.

Prepayment penalties in commercial loan agreements are common, and they are often quite large. Interest rates are typically higher. Default times are quicker. Sometimes there is not even your typical 30-day billing period. With some commercial debts you pay daily. Many also have a "security" placed on your assets and/or receivables called a "UCC-1". UCC-1 stands for Uniform Commercial Code-1 and it is a legal form that a creditor files to give notice that it has or may have an interest in the property of your business.

It is a very common occurrence for a small business to have occasional cash flow problems. Let's say you are a sub-contractor and you don't have the money for payroll because you have not been paid by the general contractor. You need to bridge the gap, so you enter the shark infested waters of lenders who will loan you $20,000 <u>tomorrow</u> so you can meet payroll. These are loans that are done very quickly, and you don't really know what you are signing. The money is deposited in your account, and payroll is met the next day. The problem is the interest rates are high, the terms are bad, and the penalties are astronomical. Even worse, you may have signed a "consent judgment" which means they do not even have to go to court because you already signed a stipulation for entry of judgment!

I had a client who was a self-employed electrician. He had a small shop and had some cash flow problems. He borrowed $100,000 and was paying back a certain amount every day (mistake #1). He paid for a month or two but making such high payments became very difficult and then impossible. Ultimately, he had to default (mistake #2). They added on a $192,000 default penalty! They sued him, but he knowingly did not respond to the lawsuit (mistake #3). The creditor got a judgment in excess of $400,000 within just a few months! The obligation was secured by his condo (mistake #4). They got a court order to sell his condo. Even if they sell his condo, they will probably only get $100,000 which means they will still be chasing him for yet another $300,000. Legal help is absolutely required and the sooner the better on commercial transactions. The real heartbreak is I could have saved him so much money if only he would have called for a consult early on.

Did my client "know" what he was doing? Sure he did. He knew it was a bad loan. Did he sign all disclosures? Yes. But did he have any real idea what they could do to him if he defaulted? No. He is an honest guy who thought he could manage it. Now he knows he really blew it. That was a very expensive lesson. It's a long and arduous process to navigate out of these waters.

Nor it is unusual for a business client to mistake a "loan" for what is really a sales agreement. Many clients think they have entered into a loan agreement when in fact they have sold their receivables. That is, they have entered into a Sales Agreement and the "lender" is actually a "purchaser". Many small business merchants regularly sell or assign their receivables. That usually means that for each dollar that's deposited into their bank account, a certain percentage is paid to the purchaser. Knowing the difference between phrases like lender, purchaser, seller and buyer are all very important in terms of what laws apply. You must be careful. You'll need a lawyer who knows the difference. One who knows how to argue those differences to be successful.

In the courtroom, business agreements are scrutinized more closely. Judges are more apt to read commercial agreements than credit card agreements. Nobody wants to read a credit card agreement. Not you, not the judge, no one does. But the judge *will* look at each commercial agreement because it's a lot less standardized. A qualified attorney will know all the relevant terms and how to represent you in these cases. We have won cases merely because the proper corporate name was not on the documents. Sometimes there is very little documentation. It could be as simple as a Staples invoice. Sometimes it's a commercial lease for space or equipment for a lot of money. Again, different laws apply to different types of debts.

Another thing about commercial debt that you need to be aware of if you are a small business is personal guarantees. The bank will require the owner of almost every small business or closely held corporation or LLC to sign a personal guarantee. What that means is the bank can pursue the owner individually for the debt, even if the company is out of business. It's just like a co-signer.

Further, even though it's a personal guarantee, it will still retain its character as a business or commercial debt. You as an individual can have commercial debts. That is, just because you are an individual does not mean it's a consumer debt. It will retain its nature as a commercial debt and they will be able to pursue you and sue you personally even though you are out of business.

The main thing to remember is to be very selective when you get into these agreements. If you're in them already, you must talk to a lawyer to learn what your rights and obligations are. Do this before you default so you can minimize the damage. That being said, we have many clients with commercial debts that we negotiate. We've negotiated and resolved those obligations for less than 100%, even with ongoing businesses.

Chapter 5

Type of Debt III: Student Loans

I got my first student loan in 1980 as a freshman in college. Then I had another one for each year of college. The first one had an interest rate of 3% and the loan proceeds went directly to the school, not to me. I also had some grants and worked through school to pay for some of my expenses on my own. Fortunately, I was able to pay those loans off because they weren't that excessive. I think I had a total of $15-20,000 in undergraduate student loans. It was a very good program.

Unfortunately, what was once a good program has become a monstrosity of higher tuition, predatory loans, aggressive collection, and excessive fees. In the time since my loans, the statute of limitations has been eliminated for Federal Student loans. Bankruptcy laws have changed to make it very difficult to discharge student loan debt in bankruptcy. Interest rates and tuition have skyrocketed.

As this graph shows, tuition has increased nearly ten-fold in 30 years. That is like a car that cost $20,000 in 1985 now selling for $200,000!

In-state tuition

Annual undergraduate tuition for the UC system (including mandatory fees), since 1989:

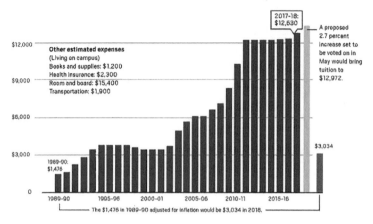

Sources: University of California and Bureau of Labor Statistics

They've expanded the scope of student loans such that now the term "student loan" means that if you're a student, you can get a loan. Almost any kind of loan, whether you can pay it back or not. It does not matter whether you are going to barber school, or engineering school, or Harvard. If you are enrolled as a student somewhere you can get a loan. Nor does it matter what type of income you may have in the future. In short, the student loan "space" is an industry all on its own and there is little to no link between what the loan is for and what the student will get.

It is not the goal of this book and it is not possible to provide and in-depth analysis of student loans in just a few pages. What I hope to provide here is some direction to students and families confronted with this debt type and lay the foundation for some basic decision making on how to address student loan debt as the part of any debt settlement plan. I strongly suggest you speak to an attorney who focuses on student loans, even if you think all is well.

THE BANKRUPTCY ALTERNATIVE

Students are typically younger in age, less sophisticated financially, and still looking to find their career. Yet they are being asked to sign documents and indenture themselves for potentially hundreds of thousands of dollars to be paid over decades. They have no idea what the impact of those documents are or what it will ultimately cost them. School finance departments will do whatever they can to get the loans for students approved. Parents and co-signers are more apt to help because it is for a "good cause" like education. They usually co-sign having no idea what they have committed themselves to.

There is less disclosures on those documents than if you buy a house or a vehicle, but many times they involve much more money and have much higher interest rates. The student loan documents also provide the consumer a lot less protection. It is not an accident that many of these loans are "promissory notes" rather loan "contracts" (this is a legal distinction that does have ramifications). Today there are millions of students, and their co-signers, on the hook for not just $15,000 or $20,000, but more than $100,000. And much higher penalties for failure to pay. This is further compounded by false information provided by loan servicers, inaccurate billing statements, and poor transaction records.

So where does one start for debt relief on student loans? First thing you must do is determine the types of student loans you have. There are two types of student loans: federal and private. Federal Student loans are either initiated by, or ultimately guaranteed by the federal government's Department of Education. Private Student loans are loans that were initiated by private lenders, generally traditional banks like Bank of America, US Bank, Wells Fargo, and others. These are owed to or guaranteed by the private lender.

The laws on Federal Student loans are vastly different than the laws on Private Student loans. The laws are so different that frequently my advice is usually the opposite for federal loans than it is for private loans. For this reason, any plan to resolve this type of debt must first start with knowing what type of loans a student has so you know what laws to apply. Most clients have no idea whether their student loans are federal or private or even some of both. This is further complicated by the fact that most student loan servicers service both types, often at the same time. These servicers often "confuse" the two, as well. They say by "mistake". I'm not so convinced.

If you're not sure what kind of loan you have, the place to start is by logging on to the US Department of Education central database for student aid at: http://www.nslds.ed.gov/. Here you can find all the data on your Federal Student loans (at least post 1999 Federal Student loans). If your loan is listed there, you have a Federal Student loan. If it's not there, it's a Private Student loan. Keep in mind you may have both types.

Most people will tell you that you're better off with federal loans. They claim the private loan lenders are more predatory and difficult. I disagree with that assessment and, subject to specific circumstances, advise families to get private loans over federal loans if possible. Here's the Good and the Bad on each type:

Federal Student Loans – the Good

- Federal Student loans are typically easier to get (which is why most do not require a co-signer). They're usually easier in terms of their payment schedules. You can usually get lower monthly payments than you can on private student loans. They allow for income-driven repayment plans, so your payment can be based upon what your income is. If you're making $12 an hour, your payment will be X. But if you're making $100,000 a year, your payment may be 10X. That helps individuals, particularly on the lower end of the income spectrum, to be able to afford the payments (at least on a monthly basis).

- Federal Student loans also have various forgiveness plans. For instance, if you qualify and you're a public teacher, it is possible to get loan forgiveness after 10 years of payments. If you work for a public entity or a non-profit, you can be entitled to forgiveness of the balance if you make so many payments. This does not apply to all loans however!

Federal Student Loans – the Bad

- Even with these advantages, you don't have any real due process with the federal loans. Other than on some very old types of Federal Student loans, the federal government does not have to take you to court. They can seize your wages or other assets "administratively". You do not have a right to a jury or even a court process to determine if you owe or what you owe.

- There is no statute of limitations on Federal Student loans. This means, the federal loan will never go away unless paid or forgiven. The federal government can pursue you until you die. I know of a case when the individual paid their loan in the 1980's and the government pursued them in 2017! The consumer did not keep proof of the payment over that time and therefore cannot prove it was paid.

- Federal Student loans can take what are otherwise exempt monies. For example, they can take Social Security and other types of benefits that are off limits to private student loan lenders.

- Here's what I think is insidious about the federal loans: Yes, they will accept a smaller amount as a payment each month. But most times, that means you're not paying it off. Your balance is actually growing. If you owe $120,000 on the loan and you're allowed to make a payment of $100, you are paying $1,200 per year. When you consider the interest on that loan, let's say it's 10%, you now owe $130,000 at the end of the year. People don't know that. They're getting further and further in the hole. You need to do the math, so you know what you're getting into. Otherwise, if you haven't paid your bill, 40 years later they can take it out of your Social Security check. That happens. I've had clients on Social Security who have a portion of their benefit taken from them every single month.

- Finally, the government can change the rules. The king can always change the rules. Uncle Sam sets the terms by which you must repay him by. A classic example of this occurred in October of 2017. In 2007 the federal government created a forgiveness plan that stated if you worked for a public agency, like the county probation department, and you made your Federal Student loan payment for 10 years, any balance remaining after that would be forgiven. Many of those people have recently been told by the Department of Education that some of those loans may not be forgiven. Consumers are being told that the loan forgiveness applications weren't processed properly 10 years ago, or that their particular type of loan was not subject to this particular forgiveness program. There are many people that paid for 10 years believing they would be debt free, and many are not going to get the forgiveness they thought they going to get when they took that job working for the public agency. Bottom line, when dealing with the government, there is no guarantee that the rules won't change (or at least be "interpreted" differently depending upon who is in power at the time).

I typically recommend that if you have a Federal Student loan and are not on any qualified forgiveness program, get the lowest possible income driven repayment plan you can, even if it's $100 a month. Then, if you want to pay the debt off, you must pay more to reduce principal. Some clients, particularly those that are elderly, have no ability to pay them off. They're going to pay the minimum amount believing that the only way you beat Uncle Sam is to die owing Uncle Sam, just like with taxes. I tend to agree.

Others just escape as best they can. I've had clients actually move away and go "underground". The problem with that is they also have to give up any public benefits or tax refunds they would otherwise get. If you ever try to access to those funds, the federal government will get them instead.

Another plan that people employ is to simply stay enrolled at a school. If you're properly enrolled in qualifying classes, you may be able to get your federal student loan payments deferred. I have clients that are taking cooking classes. Not so much because they want to become a cook, but because they don't have the money to pay their student loans. It's cheaper to go to the local college and take classes on how to cook lasagna!

Private Student Loans – the Good

Private Student loans, just like credit cards, are unsecured debt. It's not secured by anything. It's a loan between you and a private lender. The only real difference between your Private Student loans and your credit card is the bankruptcy question. (I'll get into this more later, but generally speaking, student loans, private and federal, are not something you can get rid of in bankruptcy.)

- Certain types of income and assets are exempt from attachment. Things such as social security and VA benefits, tools of the trade and others. These items can never be taken from you by a Private Student loan lender.

- There is a Statute of Limitations on Private Student loans. This means private lenders must sue you within a certain period of time. If they don't, you can never be forced to pay them. I've had clients in which the statutory time period has passed, and they were not sued. Therefore, the client paid them nothing.

- They are subject to collection laws such as the FDCPA when they are collecting. They cannot call you after hours, they cannot use profanity, they cannot communicate with you when you have a lawyer. All the tools that we use for debt settlement plans are available on private student loans (except the threat of BK).

- You have a right to a jury trial. You have a right to contest the loan. You have a right to determine what payments were or were not made.

Private Student Loans– the Bad

- With private student loans you have no right to an income-based repayment plan or the various forgiveness plans. Subject to the actual terms of the agreement, the private lender can say, "This is your payment, and this is how much you owe me."

- Your private student loan lenders can sue you in court.

Because there is generally no bankruptcy option for student loans, the only way you are going to remove a Private Student loan debt from your life is to do one of the following 3 options:

1. Pay it off. Easy to say and it depends on the amount of course. But if you come into some money–pay it off (or better still: settle it for less!) I've had parents take a loan on the house to pay off the kid's Private Student loan debt. There are more lenders willing to "refi" your student loans. The primary advantage (other than maybe a better interest rate) is at least you can get reliable data on balances, payments, etc. Be careful, of course. You do not want to convert unsecured debt into secured debt if possible. A refi may also allow you to get a co-signer off the loan.

2. Work out a payment plan arrangement. But it **MUST** have 3 things: **One:** payments you can actually make; **Two:** a set term (number of payments); and **Three:** it must be in writing! Never make payments without knowing how many payments it will be. Virtually every student I speak to has no idea how many payments they are supposed to make. All they know is the payment amount the lender tells them on the phone (which often changes inexplicably). I don't recommend anyone

make any payments on any Private Student loan unless you can show me something in writing from the lender that states the amount is fixed and the number of payments to complete the agreement.

3. Default. We talked a little about this in "the life of a debt" in chapter 2. More often than not, due to the inability to get either of the two above options, I advise clients to default.

It is not unusual on student loan payment plans that you will find: YOU WILL NEVER PAY IT OFF! Any financial advisor will tell you should not make payments on any debt without a term. It makes absolutely no sense to pay $500/mo. for 5 years, only to discover that the balance of the debt has increased. **Always remember: IF THERE IS NO STATED TERM, DO NOT MAKE ANY PAYMENTS**. You must also insist upon some sort of written documentation to that effect. If you have a payment plan, and if they're guaranteeing a term, put it in writing. If they refuse–don't do it! If you have it in writing, hang onto that, that's gold. I very rarely ever see that from potential clients, which is why I generally suggest the third option as a way to get to a settlement on either a lump sum or payments with a specified term.

I had a mailman and his son in my office some months back. The mailman had co-signed on his son's private student loans. He showed me all of his records and said, "This is what we've done on my son's student loans. We've been paying for five years, here's the proof." In addition, the dad had received a small inheritance when his own dad passed away. They took that money and they applied it to the student loan as well. He was shocked to learn that despite all that HE STILL OWED MORE THAN THE ORIGINAL LOAN AMOUNT!

He said, "I'm about to retire. At least I want to retire. I've been working at the post office for 30 years. One of the commitments I made to my son is we, his mother and I, would take care of his student loans for him. I felt it was my obligation to put him through school. But I can't retire now because I still owe as much as I did when he came out of school and I don't understand it. How can that be?" It can be very heartbreaking to see this happening right in front of you.

Here's a gentleman who has worked hard his whole life. He has good credit. He bought his home and has paid all his bills. He told me, "Greg, I just don't want to default. That's not how I work." I said, "If you want to get on a payment plan so you can pay this off so you and your son will be debt free, my view is that your best option is to default unless you can pay it off right away (which he couldn't do) or get the lender to give you a payment plan WITH A TERM in writing (which the lender wouldn't do)."

When you default, the private student loan debt will follow the stages and life described in other chapters. When you go to the lenders or the servicers, they won't give you any reliable information either. I frequently tell consumers, you're really going to have to default if you insist upon seeing the source documents. And frankly, I think they should insist!

While in the "pregnant" stage, I tell creditors, they are going to have to give us the source data if they want to pursue it. "Show me the data, and we can talk about settlement". I can say this because I know sooner or later they will have to provide it in court, which is the only way they can force any one to pay. In court they will not only be forced to provide the data but must do so under penalty of perjury. This is one of the reasons I tell consumers never be afraid of going to court.

The mailman's only real option, in my view, was to default. Maybe they'll sue him, maybe they won't. Worst case scenario is we will get a definitive payment plan in writing. But we're prepared either way. It can be a very difficult decision to default if it's not how you've done business your entire life. But when confronted with large balances, a lack of documentation, and a refusal to put terms in writing, you have little choice. If the lender had given our mailman a documented payment plan that told him the exact terms, the balance due, the monthly payments, and how long it would take, he would have done it. But they didn't. So he defaulted.

Here's a typical plan we come up with. Instead of giving the private student loan lender $1,000 a month, the client will put away $1,000 a month so that in a year he'll have $12,000. In two years he'll have $24,000. With $24,000 and 2 years delinquency, he will be able to either get a lump sum settlement or at the very least an affordable payment plan with terms in writing. That's how he'll become debt free. That's how he is going retire.

Quick case note: we had trial recently. A private student loan lender sued one of our clients. They would *not* negotiate. They wanted 100%. With nothing to lose, we went to trial. Our client did, in fact, borrow the money. The private student loan lender sold the debt to a company called EduCap, and that was the company who sued. We contended that EduCap could not prove its case because it could not properly introduce the documents between student and lender to show what the loan amount was or what the payments were. In this case they had the documents, but they could not introduce them into the court record because the records were not created by the debt buyer. They had no authority or ability to say those records were sufficiently reliable to be introduced into the court record as evidence. The judge agreed and ruled that EduCap did not produce the evidence sufficient to prove their case. They weren't given a judgement.

We won the Educap case because they couldn't introduce the proper evidence. We knew the objections to make, and we knew the argument that the judge needed to hear to give us an opportunity to win that case. If you don't know what those words are, if you don't know what those objections are, if you don't know what the evidence is or if you don't know how to authenticate documents, the odds are you won't win a case like that. If you're not a lawyer, don't pretend to be one. I don't fix my own sink because I'm sure I would wreck it. It will cost me more in the long run to do it myself. You can save a lot of money if you use the right lawyer.

Other Types of Student Loans

Sometimes we'll get cases on loans that are 20, 30 years old. Back then there were student loans that were guaranteed by the California Student Aid commission. If a lender like the Bank of America didn't get paid, the State paid them off. Now the student owed the State. The loan, in turn, was guaranteed by the federal government, so it became a Federal Student loan.

In those situations, they have to sue you. I've had many clients sued by the United States of America for as little as $2,500 in federal court against somebody who's over 75 years old. It may seem ridiculous, but they do bring those lawsuits. Those are different than your standard federal loan or your private student loan.

The point is there is a long history of student loans. Over time there have been different types of loans and many have special rules attached to them. That means there are many different types and hybrids of student loans, both federal and private, that need to be handled very differently.

Bankruptcy on Student Loans

Most people believe that student loans are not dischargeable in bankruptcy at all. This is because they are generally not dischargeable other than a few exceptions. There are individuals who do qualify to have their student loans discharged. A classic example is someone who is permanently and totally disabled. They can't go to work and are unable to get an income. They are essentially destitute, and don't have significant resources or assets.

However, even in this specific case type and unlike credit cards or medical bills, if one wants to discharge a student loan debt they must get a special order from the BK judge. This is because there is an additional proceeding within the bankruptcy case to specifically determine if the student loan should be discharged. This additional process that the consumer must use in the bankruptcy process is called an Adversary Proceeding. It's a lawsuit inside of the bankruptcy in which the BK judge will determine if you qualify for one of the exceptions to get your student loans discharged in bankruptcy.

The additional cost to do this is a big reason that you don't see more discharges of student loans.

Here's the problem: even when the exception is clear (as with a permanent and totally disabled person), the Federal government and private student loan lenders have taken the position that they're going to fight it. They can run up the student's legal fees to discourage anyone, even someone who is permanently and totally disabled, from getting the discharge. I believe they do that because they want the general myth that BK is not an option for student loan debtors to continue. They like that myth. They like it so much that they will fight every case. Even the obvious ones. And they are winning because the student has no money to fight the case in bankruptcy court! What's insidious is that those that qualify because of their financial circumstances are the same people that can't afford to get the result because they don't have the money to do it. It's a very difficult situation to be in.

"Scam Schools" Note

One last comment about student loans. There are fraudulent schools that overstate their placement policies, the qualifications of their professors, and many other abuses. They take people's money and then shut down. Students commonly state: "The school's out of business. I don't owe my loan anymore."

That's not necessarily true. It's akin to the Lemon Law scenario with vehicles. The lender, be it the Department of Education or the private lender, is going to say, "I didn't misrepresent anything. I didn't guarantee that you were going to get a job when you got out of school. I didn't do anything wrong. I lent you the money and now you owe me the money. If the car's a lemon, if the school's a lemon, not my problem. You still owe me my money." There are students who didn't even get the education or what was promised by the school. Unfortunately, a majority of the time they still owe the lender.

There may be cases when the lender decides to forgive the loan. The federal government, on some of the more outrageous abuses, has forgiven loans. Again, being the king, they can decide that they're going to change the rules which means they can also change the rules for the better. It does happen, but you don't have a right to that. It's certainly not a right of yours if you have a private student loan, unless of course, the lender is the school. If the school wants to pursue you for the loan and you have a counterclaim for the school misrepresenting itself, then certainly yes, in that scenario, your defense to that debt can be successful.

By and large, the fact that you went to a bunk school doesn't have anything to do with whether you owe the federal government or a private lender money. When somebody is trying to get debt relief and their plan is they don't owe this money because they didn't get the job they were promised ... time to get a new plan. Is it something that we use in court? Certainly. Does it have appeal? Yes. Is it legally sufficient? No, it won't work all by itself. Every day I talk to people who have student loans and at least half of them complain about the school. Good or bad, you still owe the lenders.

The essential point on student loans is that, as of this writing, bankruptcy is very rare. Your Federal Student loans are never going away so you must have a plan for them. On Private Student loans, if they are unaffordable, default on them to get a new agreement with a specified term and fixed payment amount, IN WRITING!

Chapter 6

Know the Players

What can be more important than what the law books say is who the "players" are. You must know who you are dealing with, whose "sitting at the table" so to speak. Most people wrongly think it's just them and the creditor/collector. If that were true, you would have no chance. In addition to bankers, financiers, servicers, collectors, lawyers, and debt buyers, you have insurance companies, property owners, lessors, healthcare enterprises, government agencies, vendors... and the list goes on.

There is a judge (who is not necessarily always correct but who is always "right") who is the ultimate decision maker. The creditor not only has lawyers, but others they are responsible to. You should also understand that everyone at the table has their own concerns and bias, even the judge. You definitely should have a lawyer as this is not a table you want to sit at all alone.

And not only do you have one "table" at which you must know all the players, you typically have several "tables" (debts) to deal with. Each with their own cast of players who are very adept at their own type of debt and laws. You will never know it as good as them. You literally must be the champion chess player playing several tables at once, and it's the first time you ever played chess! It's a real swamp out there and there are many different types of swamp creatures waiting to take your money including the scams who want your money (both collection scammers and debt settlement/elimination scammers). As we've seen already there are a lot of different types of debt and different laws that apply in different ways and these scammers are salivating as you enter the debt settlement jungle on your own. It's a lot to handle.

The only thing worse than an unscrupulous collector is the fraudulent "consumer advocate". Do not assume that when someone labels themselves a "consumer advocate" that they are there to help the consumer. In fact, you should assume the opposite until proven otherwise. There are many wolves in sheep's clothing and one must be vigilant to successfully complete a debt settlement plan. Even government regulators are many times doing the bidding of the banks in the name of "protecting" you the consumer.

The courts can also be perilous for debtors. Unfortunately, although many are called "Justice Centers", courts are not without bias. In fact, in over 26 years of practicing law I can say without a doubt that the most prevalent bias exhibited by judges is against debtors. Even more than in the criminal courts. Everyone, including judges, all believe you owe the money and have made up their mind just by looking at the case type (which are identified in court stats as "collection" cases). Such a term automatically presupposes money is due.

Some basics on each of these "Players" are:

Original Creditors

As stated above briefly, for debt settlement purposes, there are two "types" of original creditors. This is because California law considers some original creditors to also be debt collectors, and some are not debt collectors. It's important to know the difference because different laws apply to each.

First, you have those creditors who typically *do not* engage in debt collection as part of what they do every day. For instance, your dentist, doctor, plumber, or landscaper can be an original creditor. These types of creditors typically do not engage in debt collection as a significant part of their business. They collect amounts due them, but it's not a central part of what they regularly do. It's not their primary service. If you get a call from your doctor or relative you may have borrowed money from, different laws apply because debt collection is not something that they regularly do. Another way to look at it is they are not financial businesses that lend money and therefore do not collect regularly.

Then we have those creditors who *are* engaged in debt collection daily. That includes banks and financial institutions that loan money. There will always be a debt collection component to their business. This is why debt collection attorneys can be considered "debt collectors", because although it is a legal service rendered to a client, they primarily engage in the practice of debt collection.

Why is it important to know which you are dealing with? Because the laws as to each are different and therefore a different strategy must be used. For example, threatening your dentist with a collection harassment lawsuit will mean nothing to them and only show you do not know what you are doing. Knowing if collection harassment laws apply to your original creditor will have a direct impact on the success of any debt settlement plan.

Collection Agencies

These are companies or individuals whose sole purpose is to collect debts. They offer their services to businesses and others to collect sums of money. They clearly are a debt collector. They do so on several different types of payment models. Most do it on a contingency fee basis, but some do it on a flat fee and others on a per case basis.

They are an agent of the original creditor, working on their behalf. They do not own the debt. They're just assigned accounts and amounts to collect. The money is not due to the collection agency. The collection agency is collecting it for the original creditor or even someone else like a debt buyer. Some can be quite aggressive in pursuing payment. In fact, many of these agencies have business models that violate the FDCPA. They know they're violating the FDCPA, but they also realize that they will rarely get caught and therefore will rarely have to pay the penalty.

These companies use very sophisticated software and systems to locate and contact you. Their whole goal is to motivate you to pay them money and they can be very good at that. Training and legal compliance varies widely, and it is important to always remember that they are not working for you, even though they may sound very helpful on the phone.

Most of the collection harassment laws are geared toward third-party debt collectors like this. It is important to remember that even when they violate the law, it does not mean you no longer owe the debt. The debt obligation does not change merely because they ran afoul of collection laws. This is a common myth spread by debt elimination schemes that many consumers fall victim to.

Finally, consumers should not "count their chickens before they hatch". That is, a violation by a collection agency is not easy to enforce and get paid on. Even if successful, collection companies routinely close down and then do business under a different name in an effort to avoid paying any penalties. Do not be surprised (especially if you go without an attorney) that your rights will be violated, even many times, and you will get nothing for it. And you may still pay something to settle the debt. It is not a debtor friendly world folks and courts are hostile to debtors, even those with FDCPA claims.

Debt Buyers

Another group of characters in the swamp are debt buyers. Lenders and creditors will sometimes try to make the best of their losses by selling off some of their unpaid accounts. They will sell them pretty cheap, too. This is because the older an account is, the less likely it is collectible. In addition, the creditor may have lost rights such as the right to sue. The debt buyer is going to pay very little because they don't always have a legal way to force payment. They can however still collect on it by other means.

Debt buying can be a very lucrative business. Their business model is quite simple. They purchase debts for as little as possible and try to collect as much as possible. Some consumers will pay debt buyers the full amount of the debt because they don't know their rights and obligations. They haven't talked to a lawyer, so they don't know if they must pay or not.

Many consumers are surprised when I tell them it is a good thing if your account is sold, assigned to collector, or transferred back and forth. The more this happens the better. The collectors legal position is weakening, and the consumers legal position is generally getting better because of this. This is because the supporting documentation necessary for a lawsuit, and the ability to get those documents introduced into evidence is becoming more and more difficult for each subsequent collector or debt buyer.

Remember the student loan case we talked about? The one filed by a debt buyer? Our client paid no money because the debt buyer didn't follow the proper process. They didn't present their evidence in the proper way. Everyone knew there was an amount borrowed, but it didn't matter. Case over. Debt buyer loses. This does not happen nearly enough as some judges ignore the evidentiary requirements. More on that later.

There are many myths about debt buyers. One is that debtors do not have to pay debt buyers or that debt buying is somehow not legal. It's entirely legal for businesses to buy/sell debts and collect on them and sue in their own names. Another common myth is the belief by consumers that since the debt buyer purchased the account for 5% of the account balance, that "savings" should be passed on to them by way of a lower settlement. First, not only do debt buyers have the right to try and collect the full balance due, the business model requires that they collect as much as possible. Consumers need to remember that the debt buyer purchased a whole portfolio of accounts, many of which the debt buyer is never going to collect on. For example, assume a debt buyer buys 100,000 accounts and then successfully collects from 10% of the debtors for some reduced amount. They don't collect on all due to death, bankruptcy, unable to locate, judgment proof consumers, etc. This means the amount they collect from the 10% must cover the cost of buying all 100,000 accounts. Consumers who argue debt buyer myths to the judge (or to the debt buyer) will only lose credibility and everyone will stop listening to you.

Collection Lawyers

Most people think that when they get a letter from a collection attorney, they will be going to court. That is not always true. There are some collection attorney firms who don't file lawsuits. Sometimes you may get a lawyer not even licensed in your state contacting you. Many will try to collect without the time and expense of going to court. If they're not successful, then they may resort to filing a lawsuit to collect. It is also important to know that it is the creditor who is calling the shots, not the collection lawyer. For example, the large banks audit its collectors and lawyers to see that certain targets are being met. For collection lawyers, that can include confirming lawsuits are being filed within a certain number of days. If the collection lawyer does not file it timely, the collection lawyer will lose the client. I don't know too many collection lawyers who are willing to lose Citibank as a client because they held off on filing a lawsuit against you.

Although many collection lawyers have a bad reputation, and deservedly so, it is also true that many are very reputable. Few people go on the IRS website saying they had a delightful experience paying their taxes. It's the same with collection lawyers. You are not going to see a positive Yelp review by a consumer on a collection lawyer's website. Nor does Bank of America review its lawyers online. Nor does the collection lawyer care about your negative review. In fact, your negative review may help them to generate more banks as clients!

What should be important to you is how a judge will see that collection lawyer. Trust me, the judge views that collection lawyer as a lawyer, a reputable person doing his or her job. Somebody they have probably seen many times before on literally hundreds and hundreds of cases. Handle your own case and you will undoubtedly see that the court is listening to the collection lawyer and not you. And here is the real problem consumers have when facing collection lawyers alone: they rarely get to talk to the lawyer. Most collection law firms have many more collectors than lawyers. I've seen collection law firms with hundreds of staff and just a few lawyers. That is because the bulk of the work is done by collectors. This means you get stuck talking to collectors who have scripts and built in performance-based fees for settlements within predetermined parameters. Good luck getting through that. This is what I meant by everyone at the table having their own agenda. Even within the same office, collectors and lawyers and creditor clients all want different things. When we represent clients, we can speak directly with the lawyers. That is a huge benefit to you. On your own, you don't have anyone listening to you, possibly not even the judge. It may not be fair to be sure. However, remember that your objective is debt relief (not fixing an "unfair" system).

Judges

The most important player is always the judge because they are the ultimate decision maker. Unfortunately, they tend to rule in favor of creditors like Wells Fargo, the county hospital, or the Chevy dealer. This is because they tend to believe you owe the money. And that's because 98% of the people in front of them do owe the money and readily admit it! Case after case, day after day, they get accustomed to thinking everyone owes the money. When you walk in the courtroom, the judge is *not* saying to themselves: "I wonder if they owe the money." The judge is wondering, "What's your excuse going to be." When you want to get the judge to rule in your favor, it can be very, very difficult to get the judge to listen to you, let alone rule in your favor.

The court calls these *collection* cases. The very term "collection" presumes the debt is *owed*. They don't call them contract cases. It's not equal parties coming in to each tell their story. No, it's more like you are guilty unless you can prove innocence. Unfortunately, bias against alleged debtors in the courthouse is very real. Judges don't typically love being assigned to the "collection case calendar" and many are even hostile when they get those cases. The best you can hope for is a judge who is intellectually honest, who may believe that you owe the money, but regardless of the fact, will rule that you don't because of a lack of sufficient proof. You need to have a judge who says, "Yeah. I think they may owe the money, but the creditor didn't *prove* it." Not easy to do in cases period, let alone on cases they view as insignificant. Understand that judges are like anyone else. They put their pants on the same as you, have biases, and do make mistakes.

Even on claims that are not yet in court (the "pregnancy" stage), the impact on how the judge will rule is in play (which is why the judge is always at the table, even before lawsuits). If you are engaged in a settlement negotiation, and the collection lawyer knows the judge is pro-creditor (or even pro consumer) it will have an impact on the negotiations. This is yet another reason to have your own lawyer to get the best possible debt settlements.

Those are some of the major players in the collection industry. To free yourself from the swamp in your efforts to get debt relief, you need to know something about who you're dealing with. You must have real solid and reliable data. This is not something you can get by internet research.

You should be aware that some players can wear multiple hats. For example, Bank of America can be an original creditor, but it could also be a debt collector. A collection lawyer can also be a debt buyer. In some fields, like student loans and mortgages, it is common to have loan "servicers". They are not your creditor. These are companies that service those loans. They're not collecting on the loans, they're just processing the billing and receiving the payments, then applying the payments to the appropriate accounts (hopefully). They are not always actively engaged in trying to extract money from consumers. That all said, they can be, and many times are both, depending upon what capacity they are acting. Personally, I don't think there's much of a difference between some servicers and debt collectors, but the law and the judges *do* draw a distinction.

That's why you need to know about each of them to successfully resolve any debts that you may have with them. Each should be treated differently. They all have different motivations, different models, different protocols. For the most part, they're not immune to your threats of harassment, but it's very difficult to tag them for any sort of statutory violations. We'll talk about that more in the next chapter.

The main thing that you need to know about all these players is that they are, for the most part, very knowledgeable about debt collection. They've been doing it a long time and they're going to continue to do it for a long time. They have a lot of money at stake. They have highly trained individuals doing the collection work for them. You are merely one out of millions (billions?) of accounts.

They also have sophisticated systems and databases from which they can draw on. Don't be surprised if your creditor/debt collector has more information about you than you have about yourself. They likely know everything about who you owe, what you owe and how delinquent you are. Many clients I speak to don't even know who their creditors are, let alone how much they owe a particular creditor or how many days they're delinquent.

When you're talking with a debt collector, be it a collector at Chase Bank, or at the collection lawyer's office, they are highly trained and highly motivated because they get paid by getting you to pay them. They will do their best to use all the tools available to them. They have literally hundreds of thousands and millions of accounts and you are merely one number. After talking with you, they are on to the next call, making hundreds a day, day after day. And you have one account. Most would rather see you file for bankruptcy than deviate from their process. It's really a numbers game. And they only care about their "numbers", not yours.

Remember also, that each of these players are regulated to some extent. They also generally know better than you where those regulatory lines are drawn. This is why the best settlement plan for the consumer is having someone on their side who knows where those lines are drawn better than the collectors. You need someone who knows their weaknesses, so you can take advantage of them, settle debts faster and cheaper so you can get out of the swamp altogether.

Debt Settlement Companies

Just like any other industry, you have good and bad players involved in the debt settlement space. You're going to have some people that are honest, and you are going to have some people who aren't. The trouble is you don't always know which is which. This goes for debt settlement companies (DSCs). Some are honest, some are not. Either way, as I have explained, you should stay away from DSCs all together. This is because even the honest ones are not going to be able to provide the protections and advice you need to complete a successful debt settlement plan.

Debt Relief Attorneys

Just like knowing the type of debt you have, the players, and the stage of the debt, etc., it is critical to know who you should use to help you minimize your debts. You may have a plan, but it must be executed well. The bottom line is you need to know the process or have somebody representing you who does. Someone who knows where to find the weaknesses and defects in the process. If you don't, it's going to cost you money and frustration. When you're dealing with a debt collector you want to have somebody on your side who's at least as bright as that debt collector.

You also have to know who the players are for each account you have. You have to understand what the judge thinks (or will think) about you and your case. All that needs to go in the hopper in terms of when or how you settle your debt so that you can actually become debt free. This is very difficult to accomplish on your own.

You need an advocate – a legally trained advocate. A licensed advocate. Someone who argues these cases in front of judges regularly. Someone who knows how to approach the judges, lawyers, banks and all the other players that are involved with specific types of debts. Someone the collection lawyer knows has been successful at protecting consumer rights. Someone they know will actually fight back.

Chapter 7

Collection Harassment

There are laws that protect consumers from collection harassment. The federal law is called the Fair Debt Collection Practices Act (FDCPA). In addition, most states have their own laws. Here in California it's called the Rosenthal Fair Debt Collection Practices Act (or RFDCPA).

These laws give the consumer the right to sue anyone acting as a debt collector who fails to follow these laws. Prohibited acts include:

- Misrepresenting the amount or character of a debt

- Using profanity to collect

- Calling before or after certain prescribed hours

- Contacting a consumer directly after knowledge that the consumer is represented by an attorney

There are many more prohibited acts to be sure. There are also other statutes that govern banks, and collectors, and other business enterprises, that allow the government itself to bring an action against them. The two main federal government agencies that regulate debt collectors are the Federal Trade Commission (FTC), and the Consumer Financial Protection Bureau (CFPB). Consumers can file a complaint with these government agencies if they believe a debt collector is engaged in collection harassment.

These government agencies generally do not represent individual consumers in court. They bring regulatory actions against financial institutions that can result in fines and even shut them down for abuses. Again, remember this does not automatically mean the debt is eliminated. Regardless, I always encourage people to file complaints with one of those agencies when they feel they have been abused or mistreated.

The FDCPA is a more complicated law than some might think. There has been over 40 years of court rulings interpreting this law. Banks and debt collectors have often defended themselves successfully. The path to recovery on an FDCPA case can be quite difficult. That's why a lot of the debt collectors follow a business model that will violate the FDCPA. They're willing to take the risk because they know that most consumers are going to have a difficult time navigating the labyrinth of case law interpreting the FDCPA, let alone prove the facts, in front of a jaded judge.

It's easier and much more lucrative for debt collectors to violate the FDCPA, pay a few claims brought by the few good lawyers that have been successful in navigating the complex laws. Even then, they can pay out a relatively small sum and get rid of the problem. In addition, some debt collectors have insurance for the FDCPA claims made against them. They purchase insurance, and if they lose a case it's the insurance company that will pay the consumer.

How to Determine When a Harassment Law Has Been Broken

There are two things that need to be established to determine if collection harassment laws have been broken.

1. First, it needs to be a collection attempt by a debt collector. It may seem obvious, but there are a lot of things that creditors do that are technically not "collection of a debt" by a "debt collector".

For example, your credit card lender is required by law to send you a statement of your account. Sending you a statement, all by itself, is not a collection effort. However, there are situations when your statement might also be a collection effort. For instance, let's say you get what looks like a normal statement from Capital One, but you're delinquent. The statement may have a line that says you owe money, you're past due, and it demands payment, or they will sue you. It's no longer just a statement telling you how much you owe. It is a demand for money in which case it is a collection effort. It's critical to look for these types of violations.

They must also be a "debt collector" as defined by law. Under the FDCPA, an original creditor like Bank of America is not a debt collector (they are debt collectors under the RFDCPA). Your dentist is not a debt collector under either law. The collection law firm is a debt collector under the FDCPA, but not under the RFDCPA. Confused? Join the club. So are many debt collectors, lawyers, and judges.

There are often gray areas in the law. For example: When a client hires me, the first thing I always do is notify the other side of my representation and demand that they only communicate with my law firm. Naturally, I put this in writing to the creditor/collector. I did that for a client recently on a Discover account. Discover then sent my client a letter stating: "We got a letter from your lawyer. We just want to confirm that's what you want to do." In this case the question becomes, is that a violation of the FDCPA/RFDCPA? Is this an attempt to collect a debt? Discover would argue: "We were not trying to collect money, we were just trying to confirm our customer's wishes." They will assert that they have a very strong relationship with their customers, and they have a right to communicate with their customers about non-collection type of activities.

I would say it was subterfuge designed to confuse the consumer. The letter is trying to get around a consumer's lawyer. They have acknowledged the client is represented and is inviting the consumer to respond to them directly, rather than through the lawyer. But the decision is really in the hands of a judge, and no one really knows how they'd rule until the matter is brought to court. One judge would rule one way, one judge would rule another.

2. Second, it needs to be harassment. If the debt collector says, "you owe me money," or, "you have an unpaid bill," that's certainly a collection effort. But it may not be harassment. If you get a call a month from a collector, that may be collection but it's not necessarily harassment. Now if they call you 5 times a day, every day ... I would consider that harassment.

This applies only to debt collectors on consumer debts. We already talked about commercial versus consumer debts. You can see how complicated it gets. What type of debt is it? Are they collecting? Are they a debt collector? Is it harassment, is it not harassment? It takes a lot of time, money, and expense to get a judge to rule favorably on this.

Harassment is, for the most part, a subjective assessment. Your banker might not consider it harassment to get 5 calls per week. Someone else who's particularly susceptible might find that harassment. The court has the difficult task of measuring that subjectively, and let me tell you, many are not very sympathetic. Case law suggests that it must be more than one call a day. That is, it must at least be multiple calls a day to be harassment.

Fortunately, judges are not to apply their own standard as to what would offend them personally. At least that's not what they're *supposed* to do. The standard the judge is to apply on FDCPA cases is the "least sophisticated consumer". Good consumer attorneys and lawyers for debt collectors (and you should understand that "lawyers for debt collectors" are not the same as debt collection lawyers) will argue over what is "the least sophisticated consumer."

Let's look at the letter that I mentioned earlier, the one that says, "we're just asking if you're sure you want a lawyer", even though they got a letter from a consumer lawyer with a power of attorney signed by you, stating they are your lawyer. The least sophisticated consumer might see that as a threat, as a collection effort, to trick the consumer into responding to them. Certainly, the bank would claim that there's no way a consumer could construe it in that way.

Another factor is whether the debt collector has a legitimate defense. The most common defense is the "Bona Fide Error" defense, which is to say the collector made an honest mistake. For example: They did not mean to overstate the amount due, it was just a typo. If they can establish that the collection effort, whether it be a call, letter, or any other communication, was a bona fide error, they will win the FDCPA case. Harassment implies some level of malfeasance. But if it was just a genuine mistake, like a letter sent to the wrong party or a typo with the address, it's all "just a misunderstanding".

You can see how that defense can be quite effective for debt collectors. That is why if we can show this happened to many consumers, that would help us to show it was not just a single mistake, or a "one off". Rather it is the way they do business.

There is a recent U. S. Supreme Court decision that ruled on "intent" of the collector. The court looked at "intention" and decided it was not required that consumers show the collector intended to do wrong (i.e. purposefully overstate the amount due). All the consumer needs to show is that an act was intended, such as they intended to send the letter in the mail. Did they intend to do that or not? Were they using it as a device to fool an unsophisticated consumer into making payment? Were they trying to fool the debtor into giving them money? The Supreme Court ruled that if the act was done intentionally, like the act of putting the letter in the mail on purpose, that would be considered intentional.

Debt Validation

One of the more common misconceptions involves the concept called "debt validation". The FDCPA requires debt collectors to validate debts when consumers timely request it. The reason there are debt validation requirements in the FDCPA is so consumers can identify what account collectors are contacting them on. Many times, people will get communications from creditors, collectors, debt buyers, or other third parties and the consumer does not have any idea what debt they are calling on. They don't know whether it was Bank of America or somebody else because it just said ABC Debt Collectors. So, the debt validation requirement was set up so that consumers could identify what account or debt the collector was contacting them on. That's it.

Many have distorted this law, on both sides. Many consumers believe that whoever calls you must provide you with a copy of the contract and all the records on the account in question. Not true. A simple computer printout which would establish what account it is they are collecting on is many times all that's required.

There are debt settlement, debt avoidance, or debt elimination companies who may try to tell you, "if you just send out a letter demanding verification, and if they don't give it to you, you no longer owe the money." That is false. In fact, debt collectors don't even have to provide a response to you. If you make a timely request to a debt collector to provide verification of the debt, they do not have to respond, period. What the law says is: if the consumer makes a *timely* request for debt validation the collector is prohibited from further collection activity on the account until they provide the consumer the "verification." Accordingly, the collector can completely ignore a timely request for verification (so long as they stop collecting).

An experienced FDCPA practitioner will make this request properly and timely if possible. If the debt collector doesn't respond, we know that they can no longer collect. But often they will try to collect again anyway. When they do, NOW there is a violation. Maybe they'll make another call or send another letter without having provided the verification. That is a violation of the law, not that they did not send you the "verification". Again, this tortured trail allows for a lot of abuses and misconceptions. Unfortunately, there are too many people who purport to be consumer advocates that are misinforming people as to how use the FDCPA to get rid of their debts. Like many things in life, if it sounds too good to be true, it usually is.

What really hurts is you could have had a good FDCPA case. Instead, the collector wiggles off the hook and the consumer looks like an idiot. It is not a good debt settlement plan when you fail to take advantage of the few opportunities you have to reduce debt.

Calls to Work

Debt collectors can call you at work until you tell them that you can't take calls at work. Then, and only then, are they prohibited from calling you at work. I would suggest that you put it in writing that you can't take calls at work so that you can document this notice to the judge. You will also want to prove it was received by the collector so send it certified or have its delivery tracked.

Calls to Third Parties

They can also call third parties for the limited purpose of locating you. This is the main reason family and friend references are requested on your loan application. They can call that person and say, "Hey. We're looking for Adam." That's not a violation of law unless they already know how to contact Adam. There is a lot of abuse because many times the collector already knows how to contact Adam, but they call a neighbor anyway, just to pressure Adam. It can be difficult to prove the collector knew where Adam was all along. This is another reason why it is best to have a lawyer, because there is no doubt how you are to be contacted once the consumer's lawyer advises the collector of their representation. That is, when you are represented by a lawyer there should be no calls to you, no calls to work, no calls to third parties. If there is, they have violated collection laws. This is the best use of the tools available to you.

You should also know they absolutely cannot talk to any third party about your debt (except your lawyer or spouse). They can't say to a third party, "Hey, Adam owes us money." Sometimes you will hear messages where they use the term "business purposes". For example, "This is for business purposes. We need to reach Adam." This is acceptable. If they talk to that third person that Adam owes money, then Adam has a FDCPA case.

Common FDCPA misconceptions

The FDCPA does not apply to lawsuits generally speaking. That means that once you get sued or it's in court, court rules apply. Now the lawsuit and the litigation process laws apply (there are a few exceptions).

The biggest misconception about the FDCPA is how you can use it to wipe out debt. Let's say a debt collector calls a neighbor and says, "Phil owes a bunch of money to me." That's a clear violation. But it doesn't mean that Phil doesn't owe the debt. It just means that Phil has a claim against that collector for that call. (By the way, that claim is against that individual collector making the call, in addition to the company that he or she works for.) You can sue them for the violation and obtain money damages, but you still owe on the original debt. One does not have anything to do with the other.

That said, many times, as a part of resolving the consumers FDCPA claim against the debt collector, we ask that the debt be reduced to zero. The distinction may appear slight. The thing to remember is that you do not have a right to debt reduction for a FDCPA violation and, if the debt is to be eliminated as part of any settlement of the FDCPA claim, it must be in the settlement documents. Again, this is where a good lawyer is a must.

I recall a client we had with a Capital One auto loan. Capital One was attempting to collect and in the process violated the RFDCPA law. Our client owed more than $30,000 on the car. We had a clear violation. We entered into a settlement agreement that stated our client did not owe $30,000 anymore. That was a settlement which was much more advantageous to our client than a $1,000 penalty. The advantage to Capital One was avoiding attorney fees (both their own and the consumer attorney) and they probably thought the $30,000 was not collectible anyway. What is important to note, this did not occur as a "matter of right". A RFDCPA claim was made and a settlement reached that included that term in writing.

FDCPA Damages

An FDCPA violation means the consumer is entitled to receive between $100 and $1,000 as a statutory "penalty". The consumer is also entitled to compensation for any emotional distress, pain, and suffering, as well as any actual money damages. The consumer is also entitled to have their attorney fees paid by the collector. Actual money damages are things such as out-of-pocket damages such as lost wages or medical bills. If you have medical bills because of the violation, you can recover that as well. These penalty amounts have not been updated since the law first came into effect in 1977.

Most people don't lose their job because debt collection, but it does happen. Nor is there a medical expense usually. It can be very stressful to be sure, but not everybody goes to a doctor for that. You don't have to have an actual medical bill to recover something more than the $1,000, but most judges will want some medical documentation of injury, pain, or emotional stress.

The real threat to a collector on a FDCPA case is the consumer's attorney fees the collector may have to pay also. If they lose, the collector can be ordered to pay these fees which can be significant. It's not uncommon for a FDCPA case to have several 10's of thousands of dollars in attorney fees.

Debt collectors aren't really phased at all if an individual makes a claim against them without using a lawyer. Not only is the consumer rarely sophisticated enough to win a case like that on their own, but even if they do, the most the collector will have to pay is the $1000 and any actual damages like medical bills or lost wages. While hiring their own lawyer will cost a collector more than the $1,000, they are many times inclined to do so because if they didn't, they could get a flood of lawsuits from consumers who wrote them nasty letters for violations of the FDCPA. They would rather give their own lawyer a $5,000 retainer to defend the case. It's worth it to them. Representing yourself in a FDCPA case is extremely difficult. Heck, it's difficult for your lawyer!

Even more problematic is the sad truth that most courts don't like FDCPA cases. They see them as technical violations with no real injuries and therefore not very important. You do, after all, owe the money! You should expect to get calls. It's just a matter of how many times or when they can call you and what can they say. If the debt collector didn't put the required words on a letter, the judge really doesn't see that as being horrendous. Certainly not something that is going to cause you a mental breakdown. Remember, courts are not all that debtor friendly to begin with. That's why you need an attorney who knows the process. Once your attorney gets involved, the debt collector is more likely to settle merely to avoid paying the consumer's attorney fees.

As amazing as it may sound, for various reasons many creditors would rather eliminate as much as $30,000 in debt than cut you a check for $1,000. Remember that a $30,000 debt doesn't have necessarily a $30,000 cash value. Plus, they are going to give you a 1099-C and write off the debt and get a tax benefit!

Common types of FDCPA violations

The phone calls are the primary culprits. Like I mentioned before, this can be a very subjective matter which is why it's so important to bring as many facts as possible into the courtroom. It's important to track the number of calls, the time of day, the duration, and content of the calls. But this is still no guarantee. There is not a law that says four calls in a four-hour period is, in fact, a violation. In one court it will be, in another court it won't be. If you don't know your judges, you're in a really difficult situation. Nor is it possible to know how every judge will rule every time, let alone a jury.

Failure to identify the correct amount due is another frequent violation. Again, this deficiency can be easily remedied. Many times debt collectors say they made a bona fide error. They may say they just forgot to put it on the letter. The best-case scenario for the consumer is when there are actual misrepresentations (rather than omissions), where the collector alleges an amount due that's not due. Let's say a collector got an account from Bank of America with a $5,600 balance due. Then they add on a bunch of their own fees, like a $1,000 of collection fee, and an insurance fee, and a late payment fee. Next thing you know they are claiming you owe $8,700. That's not the debt. That's a mis-representation of the debt and a potential FDCPA claim.

Misstating the nature of the debt can also be a violation. For example, a collector stating they have a judgment when they don't is actionable. We had a case that went to trial on a FDCPA claim our client asserted against a HOA collection attorney. The HOA had got a default judgment against the client. The client was able to get the default judgment set aside after a hearing. As you will learn in the Judgments chapter, this means there is no longer a judgment. The collection lawyer wrote a letter (after the judgment was removed) stating there was a "judgment" when in fact there was none. We sued alleging a misrepresentation of the debt and won. What's interesting about this case is after we won, and they paid, the collection lawyer sued my law firm alleging that the case we filed against them caused the collection lawyer "emotional distress". A ridiculous claim of course. We won that too and they paid us even more.

All debt collectors should have a compliance department to make sure that they are following the law. But many don't. I frequently tell the debt collectors they should consider my firm as their compliance department. I will happily let them know when they violated the law. They don't want to get into a fight with a lawyer who's experienced on FDCPA cases. They will settle it, maybe even reverse all the debt, and move on. They may do this even when they believe there has been no violation. This is not going to happen for a self-represented consumer.

In my office we always give a creditor an opportunity to do the right thing. That is, we write them a demand letter that states: "You violated this. We need this." before filing a lawsuit. I will tell you that I'm in the minority of lawyers. Most lawyers for these types of cases automatically file lawsuits because they automatically create a lawyer bill for themselves that they demand the collector pay. Just filing a lawsuit alone means they've spent time, and that means they're generating money for themselves. I have no real problem with that. Heck, make the collector pay as much as possible, right? But what does it really do for the consumer client? Remember the consumer is capped on what they can get, and it does not matter if it takes two years in court or a simple demand letter to get it. Also, sometimes giving the collectors what they want, gets the consumer what they want—debt relief.

We're successful because we know what the creditor wants, and the creditor knows what we want for our clients. We have sued them before and will certainly sue them again. When we call them and say "look, I think you guys blew it here, I think you got a big-time problem. We're going to do what we must do. We're going to sue you unless you can make it up to our client". Often, it gets resolved faster and the net result for the client is the same or even better, without going through the trials and tribulations of litigation (things like hearings, deposition, etc.) Creditors and their lawyers can and will put you through hell when you sue them. You never want to be afraid of a lawsuit, but nor should you go through one unnecessarily when you can get the same outcome without it. We like to use the FDCPA as a tool to get rid of debt. And we have been able to use it quite effectively.

Chapter 8

Collection Lawsuits

If you have a collection lawsuit filed against you, you are one of about 18% of all accounts where the "pregnancy" of a defaulted account resulted in the unwanted "birth" of a lawsuit. We still do not concede however that the "baby" is ours. They still must prove it is our debt. This type of debt is still manageable, but the "life cycle" of the debt, and your debt settlement plan is now much different than if there was no lawsuit. So long as you operate by the following rules you will be able to complete your debt settlement plan.

Rule number 1. Don't be afraid of a collection lawsuit.

It's understandable to be shaken when you hear a collector say, "if you don't pay me, we're going to sue you, we're going to garnish your wages and lien your house." It scares people into poor decisions. It scares them into handing over money they might not have to. The threat alone is a very effective tool by a collector. Perhaps more effective than the lawsuit itself!

When a debt collector tells me they're going to sue my client, I say, "Great. Fantastic. Bring it. Happy to see it. Happy to see your lawyer and maybe have lunch with them. Couldn't be happier to talk to him/her rather than you". I do that because I want the collector to know that I'm not afraid of going to court. Some lawyers are, but we are certainly not among them. I also remind the collector, "There goes your commission." The collector does not really want it to go to court any more than you do. It's just a device to secure payment. Don't fall for it.

Rule number 1A, if you will, is even if you *are* afraid, don't let them *see* it. The minute they see that you're afraid, they know they have you. In the 80's there was an advertising campaign for Dry Idea antiperspirant that had a catchphrase that went, "Never let them see you sweat." That would apply here, too. Even if you are afraid or nervous, you can't let them see it. If you do, your debt settlement plan is tanking.

Rule number 2. Never ignore a lawsuit. Even if you found it in the street.

If you do not respond to a lawsuit you have just allowed a "claim" to be made into a court order that you pay (a judgment). It can now become a secured debt, growing at 10% interest per year, as well as increasing by the collection attorney's fees and other costs. You have just given them the power to garnish your wages (as well as your spouse). Big mistake. Judgment debts are much harder and more expensive to resolve, and you have just blown a huge hole in your debt settlement plan.

In a collection case you may owe Citibank the $6,000. Still, you should go to court. It doesn't mean you're going to be ordered to pay $6,000. If you don't go to court, if you do not respond, you will definitely end up with a court order that you pay more, sometimes much more. Always, always, always respond.

I often hear, "I owe them money; I'm not going to win; A lawyer is too expensive and I'm just going to put more good money after bad." This type of thinking is a huge mistake. Remember: 1) lawsuits are about proof, not "owing"; 2) You could "win". A $3,000 settlement can be a huge win; and 3) you may be pleasantly surprised how affordable an attorney can be. Especially when they save you thousands and do so on a performance-based fee.

Rule number 3. A Response Buys You Time (file an Answer in the court!)

Another advantage a court filed response gets you is time. If you ignore a lawsuit, the collector will win automatically, usually at 30 days! Once they get the judgement, they can garnish your wages and levy bank accounts. This can happen in as few as 60 days. When you respond and merely file an Answer, the whole process takes much longer. Sometimes several years. This time allows a consumer to save funds to settle for a discounted amount. Always respond. You're going to get yourself some time. And respond using a lawyer. Not only can you get a better resolution, you will get even more time and maybe even a dismissal.

Rule number 4. Do not assume that the other side is going to win the case.

You might say to yourself, "Well, I owe them money. What am I fighting for?" The courtroom isn't about the true facts. It's *not* about whether you own them money. It's about whether or not they can *prove* that you owe the money. Many lawsuits are brought by entities other than the original creditors. These plaintiffs are going to have problems proving their cases. Don't assume *you're* going to *lose* the case. And don't assume that their *lawyers* are going to *win* the case.

I tell my staff and anyone who will listen: showing up is half the battle. Showing up yourself, while not preferred, is better than not showing up at all. At least you've bought some time.

Show up with a competent lawyer, you'll get even further. They are going to give you a decent chance of, if not winning the case, certainly reducing the amount you might have to pay.

Rule number 5. Hire a lawyer.

If you represent yourself, you will have to answer questions that may incriminate you. Often it will be the judge, not even the other side, who will start questioning you. Remember the bias I told you about earlier?

I remember waiting in the courtroom for one of my cases a while ago. The scene went something like this.

> Poor Brenda is trying to defend herself while the collection lawyer was half asleep. The judge asked her, *"Brenda, did you have a Citibank account?"*
>
> *"Yes."*
>
> *"How much did you owe on it?"*
>
> *"I don't know your honor."*
>
> *"Okay. Well, they're telling me it's $6,700. Do you have anything to show me it's not $6,700?"*
>
> *"No, I don't."*
>
> *"Well Brenda, it looks like you owe them $6,700, don't you?"*
>
> *"Yes, your honor, but I can't pay it"*
>
> *"Judgment for Citibank in the amount of $6,700 plus attorney fees and court costs for a total of $8,000. Good luck Brenda"*
>
> *CALL THE NEXT CASE PLEASE*

Great. You lose Brenda. Judgment for Citibank. The judge is not going to let Brenda off the hook because she's got a great smile.

Many people who represent themselves lose the case as soon as they file their own response. Many tell the court: "I owe it but can't pay it your honor because I lost my job". It's kind of like guilty with an explanation. When you do this, you have only bought yourself a few months because the collection lawyer is going to ask the court for a judgment based upon your own court filings. You have, after all, admitted to owing the debt. What is there left for a court to decide?

Even those that may get the filings right, then get served with "discovery" by the collection lawyer and you must then provide answers to specific questions under oath within 30 days (sometimes less). If you don't (and most consumers don't) the court will rule against you, sanction you, and you will lose. The collection lawyer has just used the process against you. What you need to do is use the process against them!

The best reason to have a good attorney is that they will know the laws and processes that can be applied to protect you. Documents and statements and everything that is part of a case must be presented in a special way before the judge can even consider them. If it is not done correctly, it is not part of the case against you. This process is far too complex to adequately explain here and it takes years to learn and properly apply. As stated elsewhere, the biggest issue is getting the judge to follow the law. Some tend to follow the bias that "this guy owes the money" and ignore the evidentiary requirements. Others will follow the law regardless of outcome.

An experienced courtroom attorney can also help resolve cases before a case is heard. Many of the collection attorneys don't want to spend the time and energy in a trial. Especially a trial with a difficult consumer attorney who knows the ropes. It's too easy to get money from all the others that don't have a lawyer. Collection attorneys just want to get a check and do the least amount of work to get it. Often, I'll find the opposing lawyer before trial and say, "I don't know who's going to win, but you know what? Even if you win, I'm just going to file bankruptcy tomorrow anyway, so why don't we just resolve it? Let me give you a couple of bucks. Let's take it out of the hands of the judge, settle it ourselves?" Nine out of ten times they'll do it. Those courthouse step settlements happen a lot because every side has some risk, and as we win more cases they understand they have more risk. They know that we fight hard for our clients, we've won many cases before, and we might do it again. They become more motivated to resolve it, and not only resolve it, but resolve it for less.

So don't be afraid of a collection lawsuit. It's a process. Don't be afraid of the process. But don't think you can figure out the legal process yourself either. Get a lawyer who knows the process and knows it well.

More Obvious Reasons to Hire a Lawyer

Lawyers like to say that a *good* lawyer knows the opposing lawyer and a *great* lawyer knows the judge. There is a lot of truth to that. We fight these collection cases every day, all the time. It's not just something we do as a sideline. For the most part, these cases are assigned to the same judges in that courthouse. The judge who hears collection cases today will probably be the same judge who's going to hear them tomorrow and next month. We are constantly in front of the same judges in the same courtrooms.

Conversely, the lawyers on the other side, the collection lawyers, often are not really *litigation* lawyers. They are there every day. They file a lot more lawsuits than other lawyers, but they don't get to litigate them because they win by default. Moreover, the collection lawyer who's filing the case is rarely the lawyer who's in the courtroom. Collection law firms use what are called "special appearance" attorneys. It's an attorney who is paid a small fee per case to go down to the courtroom a few days a week just to handle the court appearance. They're usually not too familiar with the case. They got a fax or an email the night before that says, "Hey Sam, we need you to show up in front of Judge McNulty tomorrow on our Discover vs. Rodriguez case." They might have some data, but they know very little about the case. Nor does Sam usually need to know much because often the consumer side does not show or shows up without a lawyer. Sam's not really a litigator. He's essentially there because the court requires a lawyer to be present at the hearing.

There have been times when my case has been called, and I had to wake up the special appearance lawyer who was sleeping in the back of the courtroom. How can that happen? They get too relaxed because they rely on the judge to do the job for them. As I have stated many times, you cannot forget the bias of the judge, even if you know the judge. There are some good, even some great collection lawyers certainly, but most of the time the lawyer in the courtroom is not somebody with extensive knowledge about the case. This can be a good thing for you, so you want to take advantage of that and have the best lawyer you can on your side.

The essential point is you or your lawyer must know the process better than opposing counsel. You must know the law better than opposing counsel. You must know the case better than opposing counsel. The great lawyers know the process better than the judge.

And when a judge interacts with a lawyer and asks real questions, you know the judge respects that lawyer. Just because you have a lawyer that the judge respects, doesn't mean that they're going to rule in your favor. But it does mean that they are going to listen to your lawyer. That's the first step to getting a successful result – the judge must be listening. The judge must at least be considering your argument. You or your lawyer must get the judge to realize there is an important legal consideration and get the judge away from the basic facts of "they owe the money". In this way their bias isn't as much of a factor when deciding the verdict.

Litigation, to a certain extent, is an art. You have to know the "magic words". You have to know when to say them. I know that we're being successful when a judge asks, "Mr. Fitzgerald, why are you fighting this case so hard? This is a small collection case. What's the big deal?" I always respond by saying something like: "I get it your honor, it's not the biggest case in front of the court today, but for my client, it's a lot of money. But perhaps more important your honor is this: there is a very important legal issue here. The number of zeros is not relevant. It is not about $500 or $50,000 dollars. It's about everyone following the same laws and process. The plaintiff has not done so in this case. You cannot disregard that merely because the case is small in terms of dollars."

I'll go on to tell them, "I never get asked that question in a criminal or property owner/tenant case". The judge never asks me why I fight so hard for a drunk driving client. Most drunk drivers are guilty. But everyone understands that there is a process that must be followed and *followed every single time*, regardless of who is charged. They also know that the district attorney must prove up the drunk driving case. If they do not, the drunk goes free. Why should these collection cases be any different?

Another example I use is landlord/tenant cases. 95% of the time the tenant has not paid the rent. Everybody in the courtroom knows that. Everybody accepts that. But maybe the property owner didn't properly provide the three-day notice or didn't follow the process to a T in some way. If the landlord doesn't prove up its case, the landlord doesn't get the judgment. It is (or should be) the same with "collection cases". It's not about whether they owe the money or not so much as it is about whether the plaintiff has followed the procedure, the law. What I try to explain to the judge is that IF landlord or the collector has followed the rules, then yes, your honor, my client loses (assuming he owes). But it works both ways. IF THEY HAVE NOT properly followed the law, you the judge can't unilaterally decide to not go by the rules. "Besides your honor, … like you said, it is a small case... they did not get it right …what's the big deal??… we should win."

What's the Bottom Line on Litigating Collection Cases?

When there are good lawyers on both sides and a judge who follows the procedure, it often comes down to the records. We are talking about the contract, the transaction record, the payments made, charges made. The important issue is: are the records reliable? Can/should they be introduced into the case? Only certain qualified people can introduce those records in order to authenticate them.

Today, most of these records are computer generated, particularly from large banks and financial institutions. Even credit card applications in recent years have mostly been done online. Those records have to be reliable, which means their computer systems have to be reliable. This means the system must have maintenance and somebody who is knowledgeable about the systems is needed to verify their accuracy. Most times the witnesses brought to trial know very little about the systems. All they really know is that they printed it out and is says an amount due. That really is not legally sufficient in my view.

Most of the time courts take these documents at face value. That is why we always look for some discrepancy, any discrepancy. If one thing is wrong, what else is wrong? All I'm trying to do is get the judge to pause and think: maybe there is something wrong with the record. It does happen. The next thought (hopefully) is to get the judge to admit, "You know what? Maybe Fitzgerald is right. This digital record from Bank of America looks alright on the surface. But maybe there's a problem with that record. After all, it is up to the plaintiff to show me there's no problem with that record." That's when we can turn the corner. The whole point is to move the judge from the presupposition that my client owes the money, to the mindset that the claim must be proven.

When I present a case, I usually don't bring a client to the trial unless they don't owe it, or the other side has subpoenaed them to come (most times they don't). If present, my client is going to have to answer questions. She's going to be put on the stand. She'll be asked if she had an account, a credit card with Citibank. Being honest, she's going to say, yes. Did you use that credit card? Yes. Were there transactions on it? Yes. Did you make payments on it? Yes. The collector has just proved up a contract without the need for any records. This is another reason you should not represent yourself as you will have to be present and you will have to answer these questions and you will have made it so much easier on them. I'm relying on records or the lack of sufficient records to win the case. If my client gets up there admits there was a contract, who cares about records anymore? That's why I never bring a client to a trial if I can.

That all said, every trial is a roll of the dice. You cannot predict how it is going to go. You cannot assume the judge will know the law, let alone follow it. In addition to arguing the law you must be able to convey why the law is important. You have to read the judge. You have to quickly determine what they are concerned about and address it. A good lawyer must also acknowledge what the judge is never going to accept, right or wrong. If you've got a great argument and the judge just does not see it the same way, you've got to move on to your next legal theory. If you continue to beat a dead horse, the judge won't be listening. You'll just be driving yourself further and further into the ground as the judge listens less and less. You've got to adapt. And a good attorney knows how to do that, in real time.

THE BANKRUPTCY ALTERNATIVE

Chapter 9

Judgments

A judgement is the court's ruling in a case that determines if a "claim" is valid. It is, in net effect, a court order. Whoever wins the case gets a judgment in their favor. In collection cases, if the creditor wins, it has now been determined that you owe the amount stated in the judgment. If the defendant wins, it has been determined that you don't owe the money. When a judgment is entered against you, it does not mean you must pay it right then. It is just that the matter has been adjudicated as to who owes who and how much.

The judgment creditor can, however, use the judgment to get other "enforcement" orders, such as an order to garnish wages or levy accounts. For these reasons it is easier to understand that a judgment for X dollars is a court order that you owe the amount awarded. Keep in mind that if you are factually "innocent" and never had the debt, it no longer matters. If you have been found to be liable, you can be forced to pay. This also works in the reverse: if you did in truth owe the amount, but the judgment is in your favor, you do not owe it.

You should also know that a judgment is for the amount ordered by the judge AND daily interest (at 10% annually) AND fees and costs incurred by the judgment creditor to collect the judgment. It is also enforceable against the community assets of your spouse.

There are three ways that a judgment comes into existence: 1) you agree to it (by stipulation or settlement), 2) the court renders its decision, typically at trial or hearing, or 3) by "default", which is to say you did not contest the case at all (or if you did, the court prevented you from defending yourself as some type of sanction for poor conduct during the course of the litigation).

When You Participate and Go to Court–Contested Cases

When you participated in the process and there is now a judgment against you, it means that either you agreed to the judgment in writing (typically called a Stipulation for Entry of Judgment) or there was some sort of an ultimate ruling against you. Either the case went to trial or a judge made a ruling pre-trial that the case was over for some reason and it was decided that you do owe the money. Therefore you engaged in the litigation process to some extent (even if it was only to sign a stipulation for judgment). You've responded to the lawsuit in one way or another.

Once the judge enters a judgement, the case is over. But even if you lose, you do have some options on how to proceed.

1. You can appeal the judge's decision. But appeals are very difficult, costly, and time-consuming. They often take a lot more time and money than the amount of the judgment.

2. You can file bankruptcy (if you qualify) and most times you will not be required to pay the judgment. There are exceptions to this such as student loans and taxes, which typically cannot be discharged in bankruptcy. Also, you can't bankrupt judgements for fraud, elder abuse, intentional injury to another, and other certain types of debt.

3. You can settle with the plaintiff, which means you must give them some amount of money in exchange for a release from the judgment, or what is called a "Satisfaction of Judgment". We'll get into settlements on judgments more in the next chapter.

4. You can wait for the judgment to expire. That is 10 years after the entry of judgment. California judgments can be renewed, however, and can therefore potentially go on forever.

5. There's one more option that is available. We call it the 747 (as in the jumbo jet) motion. It means that you leave California. A judgement by a California judge is only enforceable in California. It is not enforceable in Texas. Therefore, one way to avoid a judgement is to leave the state. However, you should know there is a mechanism where the creditor can follow you and apply for a "sister state judgement" in the state you moved to. The important thing to know is that a CA order, or judgment, is only enforceable in CA.

When You Didn't Participate: Default Judgments

Those break down into two categories.

- Properly Served/Notified of the lawsuit: This is where you were served properly and notified about the case and you chose to ignore it and didn't respond on purpose (or at least you did not have a very good reason for not responding- "excusable neglect" in lawyer speak).

- Improperly Served/Notified: This is where you didn't know anything about the case or that there was even a case against you. Generally, this is a situation where the defendant was not served correctly. If you don't get the paperwork that you've been sued, you don't know to respond.

In the situation where you were served with the lawsuit, but decided to not respond, you are in the same situation as if you did contest the case (see options above). You cannot come back to the court later and want the case to be re-litigated after you chose to ignore the lawsuit in the first place. You are usually stuck with the result without the option to appeal, though you still have the options of settlement, bankruptcy, wait for it to expire, or the 747 motion.

In the default judgment scenario where you were not aware of the case, you do have the option of making a motion to vacate the judgment. In most default judgment scenarios, the Court did not know that you didn't get the correct paperwork. The court relies entirely upon the proof of service the collection attorney filed in the case. If it is defective (other than as to form), the court does not know that and enters judgment against you, assuming the proof of service is correct. When the service is defective, it's sometimes an honest mistake and sometimes sloppy or even fraudulent. Unfortunately, "sewer service", where the server knowingly does not serve it correctly, happens far too often.

I talk to people daily who had no idea there was any case against them and the first they learned of it is when they got levied or garnished. Or maybe they're refinancing their home and escrow asks them, "Hey, did you know there's a judgement against you?" These people honestly never received the paperwork. They have no idea that there was a case against them, let alone a court order to pay money or that they have a lien on their house! It can be quite a shock to learn this.

When there is a default judgment against you that you never knew about, there are only three ways to get rid of it. By "get rid of" I am referring to legally resolving it, as opposed to waiting for it to expire or leaving the state.

1. File for bankruptcy

If it's the type of debt that can be discharged in bankruptcy (as mentioned above, there are certain types of judgments one cannot discharge in bankruptcy), and you qualify for and complete a bankruptcy, the judgment will not be enforceable against you. This is because a Federal Bankruptcy judge has higher authority that the CA state judge who entered the judgment against you. It does not necessarily remove the judgment, it just renders it meaningless. This creditor is not required to file a Satisfaction of Judgment. They just cannot enforce it.

*Judgment <u>liens</u> are a different matter. Judgment liens are not automatically removed when successfully completing a simple Chapter 7 bankruptcy. A judgment lien is a different legal instrument than the judgment itself. A judgment lien is a secured instrument and therefore, if you intend to have it removed in bankruptcy, you must get a specific order from the bankruptcy judge. If you don't do this, the judgment lien will remain on your property. Most people who have completed a BK are shocked to learn this. I'm always shocked their BK attorney did not tell them this.

2. Settle the Judgment

This is when you give the judgment creditor money in exchange for a release from the judgement. Sometimes, that settlement will be less expensive than filing a Motion to Vacate or even a bankruptcy. We'll talk about that more in the next chapter on Settlements.

3. File a Motion to Vacate seeking to "set aside the judgement"

When a judgment is entered against you and you did not have the opportunity to defend yourself, you have the right to file a Motion to Vacate the judgment. There are 3 requirements you need to prevail on in order to win the Motion:

    1. <u>You Must Show Improper Service and/or "excusable neglect"</u>:

For there to be a judgment against you, there must be a "Proof of Service" in the court file. The court would not enter a default judgment without it. This document is prepared by and signed under penalty of perjury by the process server.

You will have to show that this document is defective. Many times, that's not so difficult. It's a factual question. Did they serve you at the address where you lived? Did they have the right address? Were you home at that time? You need to establish that you were not where the process server said you were.

Much of the problem with defective judgments is due to a very bad California process serving law which is the direct cause of many people being caught by surprise by an unknown judgment. California allows for what is commonly referred to as "Substitute Service". As the name implies, the collection attorney can serve a "substitute" and not you. It goes like this:

If a process server goes to your home or work in an effort to serve you personally but is not able to do so (you are not there or do not answer the door), after multiple attempts, the process server can leave the documents with any adult who is present (the "substitute"). The process server must then mail a copy to you at that address, and at that point you have been served! The process server must complete and file with the court an additional form called a Declaration of Due Diligence where they state the dates and times they were at the address and unable to serve you personally. They must also provide a physical description of the substitute person they gave the lawsuit documents to.

The problem with substitute service is that the process server is assuming you live at a certain address because you may have lived (or worked) there at one time. What happens is the process server is going to an old address that you no longer live at. RESULT: you never know about the case. Most people are shocked to learn about substitute service and the complete lack of any requirement that your address be verified. A very bad law to be sure, but the law nonetheless.

You should also know that if you use a P.O. Box for your address, you have made the P.O. Box your "agent for service of process". This means you have authorized them to accept service on your behalf. This makes it very easy on the process server.

Excusable neglect is where you did know about the lawsuit and did get properly served, but have a very good reason for not filing a timely response at the court. The best example of "excusable neglect" is when you hired a lawyer and the lawyer failed to file it timely. Most courts will accept this. Trouble is, inept attorneys usually won't admit to it. Other "excusable neglect" reasons are that you were medically incapacitated and scenarios of that nature. Be advised that it must be a very good reason as most judges will not be sympathetic.

However, it is not enough to merely show you were not served correctly or qualify under excusable neglect. The next two are the usually the biggest killers of Motions to Vacate a judgment:

2.   <u>Generally speaking, you must make any Motion to Vacate within 6 months of learning of the judgment's existence</u>

You must show the judge that once you discovered there was a judgement against you, you acted quickly to inform the court of the error via a Motion to Vacate the judgement. In California, that typically is within 6 months. If you don't make the motion within the six-month period of time, most courts will not assist you whatsoever. It will not matter that you were not served correctly. It will not even matter if it was not your debt and they sued the wrong person. What you must remember is when you learn of a judgment against you that you contend is improper, you are on the clock. If you do not dispute it timely, it will remain YOUR JUDGMENT. I will also tell you that some judges are of the opinion they don't even have to give you the 6 months!

When it comes to proving when you first learned of the judgment, you will have to convince a judge that you never had actual notice of the lawsuit (proper service or not). For example, if you were not served properly, but found the lawsuit in the gutter two years ago, the court is going to ask why you didn't do anything about it when you found it two years ago. If your response is 'I was not served correctly", most judges will still believe you should have done something. If you can't convince the judge otherwise, you will lose. And trust me, the court does not want to grant your motion, especially in standard collection cases. Why? They believe you owe the money! That, and they already have too many cases to handle and they do not want to add any more.

A lot of people wait for some reason and don't come to us fast enough and there is no longer a way to fight it. This six-month time frame is very critical as courts just do not want to grant motions to vacate judgments, even when they know service was bad.

3. <u>Judgments more than 2 years old will not be set aside unless an exception applies</u>

Finally, subject to a few exceptions, you must file a Motion to Vacate within two years of when the judgment was entered. Many creditors, knowing this two-year rule, will not do anything to enforce the judgment for 2 years. They will intentionally wait for that two-year period of time to pass so that you will be unable to contest it. You can see where these judgments are very nasty, and why I refer to them as "financial cancer" in many circumstances. This is because if you don't owe the money, and you didn't get notice of the lawsuit, you may still have to pay. It seems (and is!) patently unfair, but it happens all the time.

There are some exceptions to the two-year rule in California:

1) If you were on active duty. If the judgment was entered against you while you were on active duty (in Afghanistan, for instance) the court will usually set that aside and give you an opportunity to defend yourself (so long as you meet all the other motion requirements as well).

2) If you were medically incapacitated. If you were medically unable to respond, then the court will usually set it aside.

3) The exception we use most often is that our client has a defense to the case; such as when it is NOT their debt, or they are a victim of identity theft. You must establish that to a skeptical court, which isn't easy. But if you do, the court will set aside a judgment that's more than two years old to give you a chance to defend yourself. The very real problem is that it can be very difficult to "prove a negative". That is, it is hard to prove you do not owe something. If it is your debt, the judgment will stand despite the lack of proper notice to you. In the court's view, which they apply very religiously, there is no need to set aside the judgment when you owe the money. They always say to me: "I agree with you; your client was not properly served. And your client has come in here promptly after finding this out. But this judgment is four years old, and your client doesn't have a defense. Your client admits he owes Discover Card. I am not going to unwind this judgment, even though it wasn't served correctly, because it doesn't matter. He owes the money." So even in these situations, it can be very difficult to get a Motion to Vacate granted.

4) You can successfully vacate a judgment if you were not subject to the jurisdiction of the state of CA at the time of the service (typically occurs when you are not a resident of CA and do not have any business or real estate ties to CA).

5) Lastly, in 2014 a new CA Debt Buyer law came into effect where if the judgment is by a debt buyer, you have 6 years (instead of the normal 2 years) to contest the judgment.

I had a case where there was a father and son with the same name, Frank Sr. and Frank Jr. Frank Jr. had access to the mailbox and one day there was a credit card solicitation for Frank Sr. Without dad's approval, Frank Jr. signed it and sent it back. Jr. retrieved the card when it came in the mail and dad never even knew there was a credit card in his name that his son was charging on. When the bills came, who got the mail? Frank Jr. of course, and he kept it from his dad. Dad never became aware of it. Jr. could easily keep the ruse alive for months, even years. Frank Sr. had no idea his son had run up debt on the card in Frank Sr.'s name. I've seen this several times. Another classic example is the receptionist who gets the mail at the small insurance agency. Same story.

This ruse can even go as far as the courts! A lawsuit is filed but wasn't served personally (because of CA's bad "Substitute Service" law). So, when Frank Jr. got the lawsuit, he didn't tell dad. Next thing you know, there is a judgment against Frank Sr.! I've even seen a brother file an answer to a case against his brother to keep the ruse going further! Eventually a judgement was entered against the wrong party. Eventually the judgment creditor did a wage garnishment to Frank Sr., and they levied the business bank accounts! That's when dad found out. The general public tends to think that all judgments are correct and isolated errors can be fixed. It can be shocking to find out otherwise.

Twenty years ago, I think it is fair to say the usual practice by the courts was to liberally grant Motions to Vacate on the long accepted judicial preference that litigants should have their day in court. They should not be deprived of justice or a hearing or due process because of a technicality like defective service. But today is a far different world. The courts are overloaded and crowded. They have more cases than they can handle, and they do not want to re-open any old cases. Especially ones where they believe you owe the money!

You should also understand that even if you successfully get the judgment set aside, **THE CASE IS NOT OVER**! You now get to defend yourself as though you just got served yesterday. For this reason, if in fact you do owe the money (even when not served correctly), it may be best to settle rather than pay to get the judgment set aside.

A word about Judgment Renewals, Sister State Judgments, & other considerations

Judgment Renewals:

Before a judgment is 10 years old, a judgment creditor must file an application for renewal if they want the judgment to re-newed for an additional 10 years. This application is filed with the court and the court enters the renewed judgment but stays enforcement until the judgment creditor files a proof of service stating that the judgment debtor has been served with the application for renewal. This can be served by mail to the address of record in the case (many times the same wrong address from 10 years ago!). The judgment debtor then has 35 days (assuming the application for renewal was mailed, 30 days if personally served) from the date it was mailed to him/her, to file a Motion to Vacate the renewal.

Because a Motion to Vacate a Renewed Judgment is different that the Motion to Vacate process described above, I strongly encourage all judgment debtors who receive Applications for Re-newal of Judgment to file a Motion to Vacate it. Courts are much more receptive to vacating a renewed judgment than a 7,8, 9, year old judgment. Perhaps the most important fact is that if you win the motion to vacate the renewal **THE CASE IS OVER!** This is unlike a typical Motion to Vacate a judgment that is less than 10 years old! Therefore, the risk of any motion is low, but the benefits are much higher! Do not ignore an Application to Renew, it could be an opportunity for you!

Sister State Judgments:

As was stated previously, a CA judgment is only enforceable in CA. Likewise, a Texas judgment is only enforceable in Texas, not California. This means a CA employer can completely disregard a Texas state judge order for a wage garnishment. So, if there is a Texas judgment against you, it has no force or effect and cannot be used to get your assets in CA. This was the basis of my 747-motion mentioned earlier as a way to avoid a CA judgment (fly to another state).

However, due to the "Full Faith and Credit" clause in the US Constitution, the orders of one state are to be honored in another state. What a Texas judgment creditor can do is apply for a sister state judgment in CA. It is an expedited process where they file a certified copy of the Texas judgment asking a CA court to grant a CA judgment which can then be used to seize assets in CA. It must be served, and the judgment debtor does have an opportunity to oppose it, but the reasons are very limited. In truth, the sister state applications are routinely granted, and it is not difficult to get a judgment in another state to become a CA judgment as well. This is one reason the 747 Motion has limited appeal. We have fought and won Sister State judgments however, so always consult a lawyer experienced in these types of cases.

What's the Big Lesson on anything Court Related? Do not Ignore Court Dates! Do not Ignore Legal Documents. No Matter Where You Find Them!

We've talked about those that didn't know about the case and what their remedies are when there's a judgment against them. But what do you do when you have default judgment because you chose to ignore it? That is, you got the documents, but elected not to go to court.

Many people ignore lawsuits for all the wrong reasons. The biggest myth out there has to do with the service rules. People think that if they were not personally served, if it wasn't handed to them directly, or because they "did not sign for it" that they don't have to respond. **Wrong**. As mentioned above, California has bad process serving laws that help collectors. It's so bad, let me repeat: A process server can go to your home or work, *or what he/she thinks is your home or work,* on multiple occasions in an effort to serve you personally but when they are not successful, they can merely hand the document to a third party — the "substitute". They generally provide a description of that individual: i.e.: Male, 150 pounds, White, 50 years old. Then they must mail it to you at that address. Once they've mailed it to you, <u>you've been served</u>!

The process server then files documents at the court swearing to all of these "facts". The court takes these documents at face value and determines that you've been served, EVEN THOUGH YOU NEVER RECEIVED ANYTHING. What can be worse is they go to the right address but give it to someone else who lives there, AND that someone does not give it to you. I often hear people say, "I got it in the mail, but I never got it handed to me. I don't have to respond." **WRONG!**

You should *always* assume that you've been served. Do *not* assume that you've not been served. Remember, the court doesn't know if you've got the paperwork or not unless you tell them! The court assumes that the documents filed by the process server are accurate, and honestly, so should you. Better safe than sorry. Keep in mind that the debt buyer that has sued you is not really interested in making sure you got notified. They just want to file something in the court that says you were notified. Then they will wait 2 years and…voila! … their judgment is now a case you can not contest!

Another myth on service is people think they must sign something. "I did not sign acknowledging receipt of the documents" is something I hear all the time. That may be true in some other states, but it's not true in California. The process server, even on personal service, does not even have to physically put it in your hand. If he's in your presence and you don't accept it, he can drop it at your feet. Many times, they drop it at the door threshold. Sometimes, somebody is behind the door, maybe looking through the window, so they'll just drop it right there. You've been served. Remember courts are looking for ways to not re-open cases. They tend to believe the process servers because, as one judge told me "they (the server) have no dog in the hunt, Fitzgerald," and therefore are more believable. You, the judgment debtor, have much more at stake (you do have a dog in the hunt!) and therefore more reason to "lie" about receiving the documents.

Understand that the whole purpose of "process service" is how the court obtains power over you (and then can order you to do things, such as turn over money). The court obtains "jurisdiction" over an individual, and therefore has the power to order the individual to do certain things. That is the whole purpose of the "Summons" (remember you get served with a Summons & Complaint).

A person who says to the judge, "I was never served," or "I wasn't served properly," is literally saying to the judge: "you have no power over me". This of course is an uphill battle with the judge, even if it's true. You are attacking the judge's power. Most judges don't like that. I've heard judges say: "You saw the paperwork, you got the paperwork, this is America. If you get legal documents, you come into court. If you don't come into court, you do so at your own peril. Don't complain to me because you got the paperwork incorrectly." That's the way they lean. Their belief is that you have an obligation to respond. You don't get far with the judges when it comes to little technical defects, be it service of process or even the case itself.

Another reason someone might not answer a lawsuit or contest a judgment is because they assume it will be too expensive to hire an attorney. Not true. Most attorneys do not charge for a consultation. Therefore, it costs you nothing to get legal advice There's no cost to you to find out what is involved, and I do so over the phone!

Some consumers assume that they owe the money. Again, litigation is about whether the creditor can prove that you owe the money. You should not assume that the creditor can prove that you owe the money. So, don't assume that you owe it. Nor should you assume judgment balances alleged by judgment creditors are correct.

When you get any legal documents you absolutely must talk to a lawyer and see what your rights or remedies are. You should assume that it's been properly served and answer the lawsuit. Better to be safe than sorry. I think if more people knew about this, they would not ignore going to court or at least would get some legal advice about options.

What Can Creditors Do After a Judgement?

Number 1—they can put a lien on any real estate that you own. A lien is like a mortgage on your property: if you sell or refinance your property, they get paid in full out of escrow. They can, under the right circumstances, force the sale of your residence. If you're a California homeowner, and you have a judgment against you, in the right circumstances that residence can be foreclosed upon by a judgment creditor. Very devastating. Additionally, be advised that if you work out a settlement agreement, 99% of the time you are not going to be able to pay that out of escrow. That is, any reduced settlement of a judgment typically must be paid outside of escrow.

Number 2—they can garnish wages (yours and any spouse). In California, that could mean up to 25% of your take-home pay. They can also get non-W2 income. Another myth is they cannot get your 1099 or self-employment income. You might think, "I'm paid on a 1099 basis, they can't get my 1099 income." Untrue. A judgment creditor can apply to the judge, to get an order against a third party (whoever it is that pays you the 1099 income) and order them to pay that money to the creditor instead of you. A classic example is real estate agents. They get paid on a commission basis, and sometimes, quite handsomely. The judgment creditor can get an order that the agent's broker pay the judgment creditor instead. And that's not limited to 25%. It could be the entire amount that you would be receiving on your commission!

Number 3—they can seize your bank accounts and other holdings without notifying you (yours and any spousal community property). And they can take whatever's in the bank account (or even the safe deposit box) without advance notice to you. Imagine walking up to an ATM or store counter only to find out that the money in your bank account has been levied. They can also seize vehicles and personal items like jewelry.

If a bank account has your social security number on it, the creditor can get it. You might have a joint account with your children for a college fund or something. That money can be seized and kept because your name is on it. A good rule of thumb is: if you have access to the account, if you can pull the money out, so can your judgment creditor.

The other thing that most people are unaware of is that a judgment against one individual is enforceable against that person's spouse. AND IT DOES NOT MATTER WHEN YOU WERE MARRIED (before or after the judgment was entered) OR WHAT THE JUDGMENT IS FOR. California is a community property state. That means your spouse's current wages belong to you. Therefore, if you have a judgment, and your spouse does not have a judgment against them, your spouse's bank accounts can be seized, real estate liened, and wages garnished. A judgment against you is enforceable against your spouse's community property assets. They cannot get "separate property" in California. For this reason, I've had clients who have divorced so that their wages will then be separate property and not community property.

Number 4—Judgment Creditors can also do what is called a "judgment debtor examination" (and yes, this can be done to your spouse and other third parties as well). I refer to this as the ultimate squeeze job. The creditor can ultimately have you arrested if you fail to comply. That's because the court has ordered you to show up in the courthouse, answer questions about your finances, and produce documents. If you fail to do so, you have violated the court's order. That is called "contempt of court" and the judge will issue a warrant for your arrest until you comply. This happens far more than people think.

There was a case in Orange County, California where an individual was in the jail for three years for failure to turn over money that the judge believed he had. Something like $700,000 in cash. The court believed he had it. He said he didn't. The court put him in jail.

Needless to say, a judgment debtor examination is a very powerful tool of the judgment creditor. Do not ignore it. Show up with a lawyer if you can. The creditor can ask you virtually anything. They can get just about anything. Judges are very liberal on allowing judgment creditors to ask for anything. Keep in mind, the judgment is a <u>court order</u>. If you don't pay it, some judges see this as not obeying the court and typically are on the side of the judgment creditor.

Judgment creditors use these examinations as a huge threat. They can be very nasty, aggressive, and intimidating. It can also be quite effective in terms of forcing people to come up with money to pay off a judgment.

What Can't Judgment Creditors Do?

The good news is that certain types of income are exempt and can never be seized. Social security, veterans benefits, disability–those types of benefits cannot be seized by a judgment creditor so long as you contest them. Other types of things that cannot be seized are "tools of the trade". For example, if you are an auto mechanic, your mechanics tools are exempt from attachment. You must however assert your rights and get a court order that the funds or assets are exempt from attachment.

We recently had a case with a client that was in the construction business. They seized his truck. We were able to establish that his truck was a tool of his trade and they had to return the truck. Not deterred, in open court opposing counsel asked, "How much cash does he have on him?" He had $90 in his pocket and they asked for it. We argued against it because that's what he needed to live on. Fortunately, he was able to keep the truck and the cash. But other personal items are at risk, too, like watches and jewelry that they see you wearing. It's important not to go into the courtroom looking like a million bucks. I will also tell you that a judge across the hall would have allowed the truck and the money to go bye-bye.

So what can you do when you're confronted with any or all these seizure attempts? Every consumer has a right to a judicial review; to ask the judge that the levy, wage garnishment or other seizure not be enforced. It's called a Claim of Exemption. If you can convince the judge that the seizure is too onerous financially, then the court can say the collector won't get it. If you need the money to pay the rent, if you need the money to pay for medical bills, child care, those types of things, then the court can give you the money back. The court has the power to reduce the garnishment and to modify the amount of the seizure.

Throughout all of this, I would highly recommend that you show up with a lawyer. I refer to judgements as financial cancer. They can be devastating financially. Many times, they're unfair. If you have cancer, you wouldn't operate on yourself or prescribe your own treatments. You'd want a doctor to make an assessment and come up with a practical plan to cure the disease. It's the same with this.

Anytime you become aware of a judgment, you need to talk to an experienced lawyer right away. Don't ignore it and pretend like it's not there. Like cancer, your situation will only get worse unless you act quickly. See what your rights are and what your remedies are. You need someone who understands the system and all your options to protect you and your family.

Chapter 10

Settlements

A settlement is an agreement between two or more parties (the creditor claimant and the alleged debtor) to compromise an amount alleged to be due, that operates to extinguish the claim or debt. Earlier in the book, we talked about how a debt never really goes away unless it's paid in full, settled in full, or bankrupt. A settlement is a payment of that debt which would extinguish it so long as the settlement agreement is completed (all of which should be documented: both the agreement and the timely payment/compliance with the agreement).

A settlement does not mean "paid in full". It's generally referred to as a "settlement in full", and that's an important distinction for creditors. *They* don't like to say it's paid in full. *Clients* like to think that it's paid in full, but it is not really "paid in full". It's really a matter of semantics. What is important is that if the documentation is legally sufficient, it's going to extinguish the debt.

There is also certain terminology that is used in the courtroom that you need to understand and use. This is another reason you really want to have a lawyer review the documents. For instance, some creditors will say, "We will close the account." Well, closing the account doesn't necessarily mean that the debt is extinguished. There are a lot of "closed" accounts with amounts due. Creditors and collectors and their lawyers can be quite clever by using all sorts of verbiage, some of which is not sufficient for the consumer's purposes. I always ask my staff: How is the judge going to interpret this? Remember, all you care about is how the judge will view it.

You must be very careful when you compromise or settle an amount due. For example, if you do not use the correct terminology, some creditors will treat it as a payment only and not a settlement in full. They'll reduce the total due by your "payment" amount and then pursue you for the balance. It's common for a consumer to come to me and say, "Look, I settled this," but show me either no documentation or insufficient proof.

I think you get the idea: documentation is critical. A legally sufficient document will be based on the stage of the debt. For example, if it is prior to the filing of a lawsuit (there has been no litigation), a letter is sufficient on the letterhead of the creditor. You also need proof of compliance with the settlement agreement. That is, proof that you made the payment, that funds were transferred, and timely so. Just because you sent the checks doesn't mean they were cashed. If they weren't cashed, or delivered on time, your debt is not settled.

Typically, these settlement-in-full letters require a certain amount be paid by a certain day. You must prove that you paid it pursuant to the agreement. If the agreement says it was to be paid on the 30th and it wasn't paid until the 31st, most creditors will treat that as a payment only and not a settlement in full. And they will get away with it. For this reason, you should track the delivery and be able to prove it was delivered by the due date.

If you have the correct documentation, you can show the judge the written agreement and the timely payment and say, "Your Honor, this is what was done, and this means the debt was extinguished."

Settlements done in court are typically called a "stipulation" and are written to be filed at the courthouse. Those usually have language that states if you don't make the payment it becomes a judgment for the full amount, less any payments that you already made. They will also enter a stipulation for entry of judgment that says if you make the payments, the case will be dismissed.

What you want to achieve with a court settlement is to have the case dismissed. There are two types of dismissals:

1. A *dismissal with prejudice* means that the case can never be refiled again. That's what you prefer, but is not mandatory.

2. A *dismissal without prejudice* means the creditor can refile the case. Dismissals without prejudice are more common and perfectly acceptable so long as your settlement documentation is sufficient.

Satisfying the Judgement

A judgement is only settled when you pay an agreed amount of money to the creditor in exchange for a Satisfaction of Judgement (SOJ). The law requires that when a judgment is satisfied, the judgment creditor must file a SOJ in the courthouse. The judgement against somebody is not over, the case is not over, until that Satisfaction of Judgement is filed. You should always keep a court-filed copy of the SOJ once you get one.

If you make one lump sum payment, let's say it's a $5,000 settlement, and you give them $5,000 right away, they should file a Satisfaction of Judgement within 14 days. Sometimes you'll work out a settlement that requires you to make payments. You should understand however that if you're going to make 500 payments of $50 a month, then the SOJ is not going to be filed until all 500 payments have been made. Nor is any judgement lien going to be removed from your real estate until all the payments have been made. Nor is your credit report going to be updated to show a zero balance until all payments have been made. That's a distinction that most people don't realize.

In all these situations, including satisfying a judgement, removal of a lien, dismissing of a case, or settling before court, you need to have certain keywords in writing. When the judge sees these words, she's going to say, "Okay, I think that the consumer is correct." Keep in mind that the judge is often inclined to rule against you. They will be a stickler and demand that you have proof that you made all your payments on time. That is, the burden of proof will be on you to show that a judgment truly has been satisfied.

For this reason, you should assume that the wording of any settlement document will be construed against you. Assume that it will not be to your advantage. Collectors and collection lawyers are obviously highly trained and are quite good at writing settlement agreements in such a way that it could be ambiguous. Collection lawyers are particularly adept at that. That is when a debt settlement attorney on your side can really help you.

Trade Line Deletions

The trade line is the account entry on your credit report. Many times, as a part of a settlement, an individual will want their credit report "cleaned". Let's say Bank of America has reported on your credit report a derogatory that you were late and that you've been charged off and you haven't paid this debt. Consumers many times will say, "I'm going to pay it and settle it, but what I'd like is for Bank of America to now report that I'm not delinquent as well." Seems reasonable. The trouble is, Bank of America cannot, by law, now suddenly say that you were not delinquent when in fact you were. That would be a false statement. Creditors cannot report inaccurately, for the good or the bad. They can't suddenly say you were current all along because that is not accurate.

What a creditor can do is report *nothing*. They can *delete* the entire entry. They don't have to say anything, good or bad. It's just that if they're going to report, it must be 100% accurate. We will often ask a creditor to delete the trade line so it says nothing because that benefits the consumer.

Unfortunately, banks will not delete trade lines. They rely on credit reporting for their lending business, so they always say that they will not delete anything. You will have more success with debt buyers, collection agencies and others. They will sometimes seek additional monies as part of the settlement in order to do so. In any event, a trade line deletion can be very difficult to obtain and sometimes impossible, depending on who the creditor is.

In a recent development (July 2017) the big three credit reporting agencies have stated they are no longer going to be reporting judgments on credit reports. This is great news. The reason they did it? They said it was because the judgment data was not sufficiently reliable. I agree.

Zombie Debts

One other thing that you need to be aware of on the settlement side is something called a "zombie debt". This is when a debt that has been paid/settled just won't go away. It may have been resolved. It may have been extinguished. And yet, somehow, a collector keeps trying to collect on it. It's amazing how much this happens. I have personally settled debts, documented them, paid them timely, only to get another collection letter stating, incorrectly, "your client owes this money." I have even settled lawsuits where a case was dismissed and then they still did a wage garnishment. That's totally improper and illegal, but Zombie debts, like "real" Zombies can be hard to kill.

These can be clear violations of the Fair Debt Collection Practices Act. When they collect a debt that's not due and take those kind of actions, the collector can be sued for violating the FDCPA. It's happened to my clients far too often. We know the case is resolved with the creditor and yet the creditor will still try to collect on the account. The client will come to me and say, "You told me you settled it Greg, but Bank of America is still calling me stating I owe money." I caution them not to believe Bank of America. Believe their lawyer because I will have all the proper documentation. I actually get excited because it means Bank of America will soon be making a payment to me and my client for the RFDCPA violation.

Unfortunately, zombie debts are more prevalent than people think. That's why it's very important to keep your documentation *forever*. Remember, the debt is never extinguished unless it's paid in full, settled in full, or bankrupt. 20 years later you can get a call that says you owe them money. This is not something you can get rid of after seven years or 10 years. If you've resolved a debt for less than 100%, you must keep that documentation because it comes back more often than people think.

1099-C's – Settlements as Income

It's very important to know that debt settlements can affect your taxes. When you have a debt settlement and a portion of the debt is "forgiven" or "cancelled", the IRS wants to know about it because *cancelled debt is considered income*. Let's say it's a $10,000 debt and you settle it for $4,000, which means $6,000 of the debt has been canceled or forgiven. The creditor is supposed to issue you a 1099-C for the portion which is forgiven ($6000 in my example). The C on the tax form stands for cancellation.

Therefore, if you get a 1099-C, you should include it on your tax return. The good news is you got a settlement. The bad news is you may have to pay taxes on the amount of debt cancelled. Few consumers actually pay an additional tax because there is also IRS Form 982 Insolvency. If you qualify, you don't have to pay the taxes. Whether or not you owe taxes is a question for your tax preparer and depends entirely on your specific tax return.

If that's not bad enough, what can also happen is that you can get a 1099-C and STILL OWE THE DEBT! Using my $10,000 debt example, if the creditor cancels the whole $10,000, you may get a 1099-C for $10,000. That is, they write the whole thing off. You didn't settle it, but they forgave the whole amount, and so you get a 1099-C for 10,000 bucks that you must put on your tax return. Now, amazing as it sounds, the collector still may be able to still collect the full $10,000. The consumer is forced to pay taxes on what's purported to be a cancellation, and then the creditor can still pursue you for the $10,000. Amazing! If you find yourself in this situation, you must get a lawyer. It is rare, but it does happen. Just know that a 1099-C does not automatically extinguish the debt.

What you need to be aware of is that if there is a settlement, the creditor can issue a 1099-C. 25 years ago I rarely saw any issued. But that is slowly changing. Now, I see a 1099-C issued about 50% of the time when a debt is settled. I do expect that to grow and expect that the time will come when creditors will issue that document on every single settlement.

When Is Your Credit Report Updated?

Entering into a settlement agreement is not what updates the credit report. Your credit report will be updated when you make your last payment of the settlement. The creditor will only report a settlement in full with a zero balance due on the account after all the settlement payments are made.

So if you make one lump sum payment, it's updated faster, naturally. If you're making payments over 36 months, even if that's 50% of the entire balance, your credit report will still show, for the next 36 months, that you are delinquent on the full balance.

Chapter 11

Should You Do It Yourself?

I am a proponent of doing things myself ... if I can. I've also learned that there are a lot of things that I *think* I can do that I *can't* do, or at least not very well. And sometimes when I do it myself, it costs me more than if I had hired a professional to do the work in the first place. Sometimes you just need help. And resolving matters such as these are not like fixing one's own car or planting shrubs. These are very complex legal and financial matters involving banking, credit, and courts. My God, we are talking about using legal tools to get big banks to take less than you owe!

Maybe you find yourself in debt right now. You're making the minimum payments regularly, you're paying the interest, but the best you can do is keep up with the minimum payments. You are just "treading water" as they say. You might even feel like you're sinking. Some are sinking and need a life raft right now, others are not sinking but are on the treadmill, literally hoping for a change for the better financially. You don't want to find yourself in the exact same position 5 years from now, or worse. What you need is a plan to eliminate that debt, one way or another.

When I look at unsecured debt I see a hole. It doesn't matter if it's $10,000 or $50,000 deep or even more. And it's your hole. $10,000 to some people is a whole lot more than $50,000 to someone else. To crawl out of that hole you need a plan. Every good plan starts with educating yourself. It may sound cliché, but knowledge *is* power. That's what this book is designed to do. It's sort of an overview of the entire area of debt settlement. Who the players are, the life of a debt, the stages of debt, the consequences of debt, the tools that you have available to you, your obligations, and so on. I hope you have found it useful.

There are a lot of financial consultants, good and bad, who will happily give you some general information about your finances and how to be frugal or save, and how to avoid the traps. But what do you do if you are already snared in the trap? That is who this book is for. I believe that being better informed about the law is always good. If you're unable to meet your financial obligations, you ***must*** talk to a lawyer experienced in all the debt relief options. If you are barely meeting your obligations, you ***should*** talk to a lawyer, and sooner than later because you are only one financial set back from disaster.

Financial advice will help you learn how to make more income, spend less, and save money. There is certainly a place for financial advice so you can learn how to budget and plan for your future. But this book is about getting you the information you need when it may be too late. When you aren't systematically paying your debts off and you need a new approach. You need to know what your creditor's rights are, in addition to your own. What can they do to you? How long do you have? How do the dominos fall and what can you do about it? You need to know, really know, not just *think* you know, what will happen and what your options are.

If you really want to get out of debt, if you really want to avoid BK, you can't pretend. You can't be in denial. You can't wish the laws were different or the court less hostile. You can't start to believe your own hype about how you got there or that you are a victim. Once you overcome these obstacles, you know that you're ready to develop a plan.

Any debt relief planning must start with a bankruptcy versus debt settlement analysis. Even if BK is the furthest thing on your radar, what's wrong with learning something about it? If you're going to eliminate your debt, if you're not able to get rid of this hole by paying it in full, then you should at least compare the benefits and disadvantages of each.

Bankruptcy

Bankruptcy, as I mentioned above, is the fastest, easiest, simplest, least expensive way to eliminate debt. And you will recover in time. Creditors love people after bankruptcy for three main reasons:

1) They know that you've eliminated all your other creditors. The odds are pretty good that you will be able to pay this new loan.

2) They get to charge you much more interest because you have a bankruptcy on your credit.

3) They know that if you have a recent bankruptcy on your record, you can't re-file for eight years. If they loan you money six months after you file a bankruptcy, you won't be able to get rid of them in bankruptcy for seven and a half more years.

Creditors are eager to loan money after a BK because you're a good target as a debtor. If you are considering a bankruptcy, I would never recommend that you do it on your own. You must have someone who can make sure that you are qualified for bankruptcy, and someone who knows the process so that you are properly represented.

Debt Settlement

Debt settlement is a much more difficult road. One advantage is that since you're going to give your creditors money, your credit score isn't affected as badly as it when you file for bankruptcy. In bankruptcy, you give them zero dollars. In debt settlement, you give them some money as a compromise, so it will cost you more total dollars out of your pocket. That all said, your credit score should not be the determining factor between filing bankruptcy or debt settlement. The determining factor should be if you qualify for bankruptcy or not. That, again, requires a lawyer competent in both bankruptcy and debt settlement.

Debt settlement is generally reserved for people or debts that don't qualify for bankruptcy, where bankruptcy may be overkill, or they have a significant moral objection to bankruptcy.

I was recently talking with a woman who was $50,000 in debt. We figured it would take approximately $25,000 to resolve that on a debt settlement plan. The next thing we had to determine was her budget. She could save $1,000 a month if she did not make the monthly debt payments. In 24 months, she'll have $24,000. It would take approximately two years for her to resolve all her debt with a debt settlement plan. It's a good plan, a solid plan. It'll work so long as she continues to save $1,000 a month towards those settlements. But you can see how it's much more financially strenuous. It takes a longer period of time. It's more stressful. Once you come out on the other side, there's a great deal of relief and pride.

Debt settlement certainly has its place, and you need to determine whether it's for you or not. Given the risks and difficulty, this determination should only be made after consulting with an experienced lawyer who has did it before. Over the years I have been privileged to watch many clients become debt free when they had a realistic plan.

Should I Use a Lawyer for Debt Settlement?

The next question on debt settlement is, "Do you use a lawyer or not?" Many people will try to do debt settlement for themselves. Sometimes they'll be successful. The creditors may even send you a letter when you're delinquent making offers of 30, 40, 50% settlements. The month of March and April can be a very good time for debtors in terms of settlements. Creditors know that consumers are anticipating tax refunds. They're assuming that people are going to get a tax refund. They encourage people to use those refunds to pay off their debts, and they often use settlements to entice them. I encourage you to pay off those debts in that way if you can. Don't do it in a haphazard way though. Do it Smart.

For example, don't take advantage of that 40% Discover offer letter when you have $30,000 in other debt and you're going to file BK anyway. What you will have paid to Discover was a complete waste. When you get that offer letter, talk to a good lawyer about an overall debt relief plan. That money may be better spent on a BK. Or, an even better deal may be available from Discover! Or maybe you can settle two other accounts. Point is: Get advice.

Good advice from someone who knows. It really is very easy to do so these days.

The reasons to utilize a lawyer are many. A good lawyer has a lot more knowledge than you or any DSC. A good lawyer knows the legal process and what you must consider if you enter into a debt settlement plan. A good lawyer has knowledge about the settlement language, the settlement documents, and what needs to be done. A respected lawyer is already known and trusted by the court, the opposing lawyer and the collectors. As a consumer acting on your own you have no reputation or perhaps worse, a bad reputation. They already know that you have defaulted on your debt. They consider you as unreliable and not trustworthy.

When you act on your own, most of the time you are talking to a frontline collector. And frequently you are talking to several different ones on different accounts. You are usually speaking with a collector who has a script and a certain set of parameters. You don't know those parameters or how you can get around them. When you hire a lawyer, they are usually communicating with somebody higher up the chain in the creditor's office. That might even mean one of their lawyers. There is a huge learning curve when a consumer attempts to settle their own debt. Learning curves can be expensive. That means more time and money that you don't have.

The lawyer obviously offers FDCPA protection. As I mentioned earlier, most consumers don't really don't know what harassment is or what's enforceable. The collector does. They are highly trained and very motivated. They work for a well-funded organization. If they have crossed a line while collecting, you must document it and be able to present that case to a judge. Just because there has been a technical violation doesn't put money in your pocket or relieve you of debt. It can be a long, expensive road to traverse on your own.

The FDCPA protection is a barrier or wall between you and the creditors that you absolutely should take advantage of. It's a very effective tool with proper representation. Not so much when you go on your own or use a debt settlement company. Debt settlement is time consuming and emotional. For most, the inability to pay their creditors is very embarrassing. They don't like to talk about it. They surely don't like to argue about it with collectors on the phone who are usually unsympathetic. It's a very draining process when you do it yourself. I know, because I did it for myself. And I'll tell you, I was not as good doing it for myself as I am doing it for someone else.

In addition to the FDCPA tool, a lawyer obviously has the litigation defense tool. I often speak to consumers who went with a debt settlement company, but then got sued. They are usually very upset that they did not settle the account before they got sued. Now they can't assist other than to say, "Well, let's just set up a payment plan on the entire balance." So they didn't even provide any debt relief in their recommendation. The ability to defend lawsuits and go to court is huge. And again, that's not something that you should do yourself.

The threat of bankruptcy is something that a good debt settlement lawyer uses regularly and quite effectively against creditors. The creditor knows that the debt could be wiped out. When debtors threaten bankruptcy on their own, collectors often don't take it seriously. They hear it all the time. They say, "Great. Have your lawyer call me." So you're better off if your lawyer is the *first* one calling them, saying, "Look, I want to work it out, but you know, if you demand too much, if you seek too much, then we'll just file bankruptcy." That has much more teeth to it because creditors know that it might really happen.

Your lawyer is going to be all about the documentation (as mentioned in chapter 10 about settlements). Contacting the creditor, making those efforts, all that documentation, you're going to have to have it all in a file in case you need it for court. You want to have it organized in such a way that you can show it to a judge. I document every correspondence assuming that a judge will see it. Proper documentation, to a court standard, is critical.

So, do you do it yourself or do you use a lawyer? It's clear you are better off using a good lawyer IF it didn't cost anything. The decision really is: how much better off am I by using the lawyer weighed against how much lighter is my wallet? How much time am I going to spend on this and how many mistakes am I going to make doing it myself? How much is that going to cost me? How much better are the lawyer settlements going to be? Ask the lawyer this. Ask to see client reviews. Ask to see case results. Ask them about the value they bring? Ask the lawyer about the fee. Is it fair and reasonable? When and how do I pay it? So long as the fee is fair and reasonable, it's a no brainer.

My recommendation is that you at least *talk* to a lawyer for advice. They'll know whether you qualify for bankruptcy or not. That will be an important decision. Even if you qualify, you may elect not to. You may decide to try to pay as many of your bills as possible, and that's perfectly fine. But you should make a conscious decision. A well-informed decision. If you don't get that kind of information, you're really setting yourself up for failure.

Doing it yourself means that you're going to have to talk to the creditors. And they will suck up your time. Lots of it. It can be brutal. It means you're going to have to document it yourself. It means you're going to have to be prepared for a lawsuit yourself. It means you're going to have to answer and prepare legal documents in the courthouse and show up in front of the judge. A judge who may not be very understanding of your circumstances. You're going to have to try the case yourself. That would be like trying to perform surgery on yourself. You would never even think about that, so you should never try to represent yourself in a legal matter (even if you are a lawyer).

If it goes further and there's a judgment, it gets even more complicated. It only gets worse the further you go down the legal process. Many lawyers are not familiar with judgment enforcement. We have many clients that come to us from lawyers that send them to us. Lawyers who represented them, lawyers who tried the case and lost the case, and now the client is saying, "Well, how do I pay it? How do I manage the judgment?"

You also want a debt settlement lawyer who does bankruptcy. There are debt settlement lawyers who don't do bankruptcy and there are bankruptcy lawyers that don't do debt settlement—so find out! Creditors, banks, collection lawyers, debt buyers, everyone on the other side, knows which attorneys file bankruptcies and which don't.

Finally, you should know that a lawyer has a fiduciary duty to you. Their obligation is to their client first, not to themselves. I must do what's in the best interest of my client even if it is to my detriment as your lawyer. That is not the case with debt settlement companies. Your lawyer always has a higher legal obligation to you.

Conclusion

Knowledge is power. If you have cancer, you learn as much as you can. You find the best doctor you can. You and your doctor will create a plan to fight it. That plan involves treatments that are designed specifically for you.

The same is true with debt relief. Your situation is unique to you: your income, your assets, your creditors, and amounts due are all unique to you. That's why you need to get more information and start to change the way you view your finances. You can continue to make minimum payments, struggling while hoping to get more money – somehow. Or you can start investigating how you can become debt free. Once your debt-free, you can start to save some money. Only then can you turn around your financial circumstances.

Your first step is to gather information. Talk to knowledgeable people. List your debts. Identify who it is that you owe. Write down the amounts that you owe. Track how delinquent you are. It's difficult to do. You've probably procrastinated because you don't want to look at it. You don't want to even think about it. That's exactly how I felt. But you can change that and say, "Okay. It's time to start thinking about it. I'm tired of stressing about it and not coming up with a practical plan. I don't want to be in the same financial distress five years from now."

If you want to become debt free, I encourage you to look down the road and start creating a plan. It you do, today's pain will be a little more tolerable because you will begin to see that there's hope. You should start the process by looking for a good attorney. When you do, here are some questions that you will want to ask.

- Have you ever tried a case such as mine before?

- Is this type of case your primary practice area?

- Have you had a case against this creditor before?

- Have you had a case against this lawyer/collector/bank before?

- What do you believe would be a successful outcome?

- How long have you been practicing law?

- How long are these types of cases?

- Have you had any disciplinary actions by the state bar?

- Do you do debt settlement, debt defense, collection harassment, and bankruptcy cases? If not, why not?

- Do you do discovery on these cases?

- Does your fee include a trial of the case?

Take it from a guy that has been in your shoes. A guy that made a plan and got out of serious debt. I know how this works and I know the players. We've been doing it such a long time that even some collection lawyers have sought my advice—not only for their own practices, but their families. I've had collectors refer clients to our office. We have clients today that work in collection offices. I consider it high praise when your opposing side sends their family to you. That's because they know we are honest, reputable, and know what we are doing.

If you'd like to talk about your situation with someone on our staff, we'd love to hear from you. We are easy to reach, and you can online chat, text, call, or email us without any obligation via our website: www.DebtorProtectors.com. There you'll find information about different types of debts and different types of results. You'll be able to watch a variety of videos on various issues that debtors are confronted with. We even have a newsletter that discusses different issues in the debt world.

The most important thing you can do is set an appointment with our office and talk to us about your situation. Most appointments are *free*. We will help identify your circumstances and will enable you to develop a plan to become debt-free.

Finally, please keep in mind that I know what you're going through. I created a plan for myself, executed the plan and got out of debt. I have a house payment, but other than that, my vehicles are paid off, my credit cards are paid off every month, and everything else is paid off.

I've helped of thousands of others just like you. If you find yourself in a situation where you are needing help, give me a call. I'd be happy to talk with you to answer any questions you may have.

About the Author

Greg Fitzgerald has always been dedicated to protecting individuals and small business from the substantial and unfair overreach of the government and its protected insiders such as banks, insurance companies, and other large crony corporate interests such as debt buyers and collectors. In nearly 27 years of practice, he has represented thousands of clients, tried hundreds of cases, and secured countless victories for his clients.

Greg is married, has two sons, three dogs, and three cats. He lives in Santa Ana, California. For recreation, he enjoys golf, hiking, and family. He considers himself to be a libertarian, a Lutheran, and very fortunate to be able to live and work in California.

Made in the USA
San Bernardino, CA
04 May 2018